Evil

Evil

Selected lectures by

Rudolf Steiner

All lectures translated or revised
by Matthew Barton

RUDOLF STEINER PRESS

Compiled and edited by Michael Kalisch

Rudolf Steiner Press
Hillside House, The Square
Forest Row, RH18 5ES

www.rudolfsteinerpress.com

Published by Rudolf Steiner Press 1997
Reprinted 2003

Originally published in German under the title *Das Mysterium des Bösen* by Verlag Freies Geistesleben, Stuttgart, in 1993

A catalogue record for this book is available from the British Library

ISBN 1 85584 046 4

Cover by Andrew Morgan
Typeset by DP Photosetting, Aylesbury, Bucks
Printed and bound in Great Britain by Cromwell Press Limited, Trowbridge, Wiltshire

Contents

Editor's Introduction

What is evil—how does it arise? What is the sense in it? Over thousands of years such questions have increasingly come to trouble humanity, as our consciousness gradually felt itself more and more cut off from an immediate experience of divine worlds of the spirit. At different periods people asked this question in different ways and found different answers. Originally the ancient sources of wisdom, the Mysteries, gave voice to it; after their decline, philosophy and then theology took on the task of seeking answers in ideas about the nature and origin of the cosmos and the human being. Nowadays we also have psychoanalysis, behavioural research, sociology, biology—all of these try in their own particular way to draw parameters round the problem of evil, or to relate it to a specific context of determining factors. Accordingly, what was once a spiritual concern has been transposed to a level of physical, external 'behaviour'. Nowadays we speak of 'aggression', 'death-urge', 'frustration', etc., and identify evil, perhaps, with the destruction and decline in society or the environment that is caused by human factors. Yet by confining it to human deeds we actually muddy our perception of its real nature and origin. Many people are content to take a reductionist view of evil, thinking of it simply as a basic and necessary aggressive 'drive' that has just got out of hand.

But evil cannot be confined within an ordered schema. We could, in fact, define it as the total absence or destruction of order—and so we seem to be helpless in the face of it. Christian theology, still to some extent modelling itself on the Middle Ages, makes attempts to harmonize evil's irrefutable reality with an image of God endowed with absolute goodness *and* power *and* wisdom; and fails, since its only reliable tool—

speculative and self-transcending human reason and intelligence—cannot unite these two contradictory ideas. The question remains unsolved—we seem to be caught on the horns of a dilemma, entangled in contradiction. There is a tendency in theological circles to dismiss the idea that the source of evil might actually be spiritual *beings*. People wish to wave good riddance to all the devils and demons which populated medieval consciousness, and to justify doing so cite all the injustices and wrongs which occurred as a result of such ideas. Biblical and mythological images of evil beings and fallen angels are said to be just 'metaphors'. This does not, though, tell us how these metaphors arose in the first place (Haag,[1] 1990). Once the idea of evil beings has been dismissed, all that we are left with is an attempt to explain evil as an effect of human 'freedom', of the 'Original Sin' which came about when we turned away from God at the Fall. But no one can explain, in turn, the cause of this. The human being is therefore left to shoulder an enormous baggage of guilt by himself, and still the ancient question remains unanswered: how can God allow evil to happen if he is omnipotent and the epitome of absolute goodness?

If we look back over the evolution of our ideas on the origin of evil, we can draw out seven basic themes from the multiplicity of answers that have been suggested (Schroeder,[2] 1984):

1. Evil does not exist; it consists only in a *negation* of good. This interpretation is still widespread today, and is preserved in particular turns of phrase. Its most important proponent was the Church Father St Augustine.
2. From the beginnings of time there have been two primal, opposing principles at work in Creation—good and evil, light and dark. This view, which originated in the ancient culture of Persia, is nowadays more or less dismissed.
3. The All-Creating God himself brought forth evil, so that greater good could emerge from it; or, otherwise, so that

human beings could be punished and educated when necessary.

4. Evil and good are two forces inherent in God *himself.* In the Jewish Cabbala, God was depicted dispensing love and grace from his right hand, while his left poured down on to humanity a punishing severity and anger.
5. The chief cause of evil is the fall of angel beings from unity with the will of God. This view became a firm belief in Catholicism, although it is now widely disputed (Haag,[1] 1990).
6. Evil has its roots in the imperfection of Creation. Matter is the most imperfect 'level'; as a 'shadow-image of perfect being' it is furthest removed from true reality. This is why evil resides in the material realm.
7. The human being is the cause of evil. Kant ascribes to the human being an innate yet also self-caused tendency to 'radical evil' alongside his equal disposition towards goodness. This leaves us caught in a duality, a choice of either/or. Hegel, in contrast, comes to the very deep conclusion that the origin of evil lies in our capacity for knowledge, since it is this which brings about a fundamental split between us and the world.

It is of course beyond the scope of this introduction to go into more depth on these seven theses, to show both the positive influences and limitations of each, or even to just give examples. My intention here is to fill in the background against which a view and description of evil's nature, origin, future and purpose can be given by an anthroposophically orientated science of the spirit. If we turn our attention to Rudolf Steiner's discussions of this theme we gradually become aware of an ever-widening panorama: he returns again and again to the problem of evil, continually illuminating new aspects of it until we realize that the theses I have mentioned are as fragments of a mutually enhancing whole, and that the science of the spirit is alone in taking into consideration the entire multiplicity of views. So we can recognize the separate theses once more, but not presented as an opposing dialectic. And we can sense this to be a real resolution and redemption of the purely logical ponderings of theodicy,* which got stuck either in the cul-de-sac of irresolvable, abstract contradiction; or—in the case of science—in a reduction of evil to an unreal and relative concept.

I would like first to highlight some of the main ideas which distinguish the science of the spirit from other views of evil's nature and origin. One of the central threads of Rudolf Steiner's 30 years or so of work developing anthroposophy was to find a *new* approach to the problem of evil that was right for contemporary consciousness. The science of the spirit has its source in spiritual experience and investigation, and does not try to use logic and reason to squeeze a few more drops of meaning out of old, dried-up traditions preserved in documents such as the Old and New Testaments. Instead it shows us ways in which we ourselves can experience such meaning; and in the case of evil, how we can experience its reality and *being*. For one of the most significant insights of the science of the spirit is precisely—and here we would already have to distance ourselves from the first thesis—that evil is not just a negation, an absence, but an actual, differentiated embodiment of spiritual realities. Who, after Auschwitz, atom bombs and goodness knows what other phenomena of the twentieth century, could rest content with an Augustinian view of evil as a mere 'deprivation of good' (*privatio boni*). We are much more likely these days to come to the conclusion that evil is the *only* reality. Some people will not be satisfied with the relativistic view which sees 'so-called evil' as just an aggressive urge, or which becomes resigned to it—in the case of suppression of civil liberties—as the 'necessary evil' of a beneficial social order. Such people will be open to the idea that we can only find the origin of evil by recognizing the *reality of the spirit*, first

* 'Vindication of divine providence in view of existence of evil.' *OED*.

and foremost through the reality of our own spiritual nature. Through this reality we can find the actual sources of hatred, violence, arrogance, selfishness, etc., even though we first see these forces as manifestations in the material world. It is pointless to talk of good and evil in the purely physical world. This vocabulary only has a sense where spiritual ego-beings—human beings—encounter one another.

There is no doubt that people seeking the sources of morality and goodness are less and less easily fobbed off with received traditions and schematic ideas and constructs about what is 'right and proper'. We are increasingly faced by the need to solve problems which have never been faced before, which have no precedent. Tradition is no help. What we need is to have an actual experience ourselves of what is good or bad. We need a perception and understanding that derives from the present moment and situation.[3] The science of the spirit provides us with the means to attempt such a task. The present selection of lectures drawn from Rudolf Steiner's complete opus has the aim of pointing the way, one which everyone can follow, to a knowledge and understanding of evil. But it cannot take the reader to the end of this journey—he himself will have to pursue the questions and paths of practice which these lectures may stimulate in him. Related themes will be indicated along the route. The theme of evil is by no means just an 'unpleasant' aspect of an otherwise positive anthroposophical view of the world; rather it is a corner-stone which contains the deepest impulses for self-knowledge and knowledge of the world. Only through understanding the origin of evil and its manifestations can we begin to 'perceive our true humanity', which is the aim anthroposophy strives to embody.

It is, after all, possible in a certain sense to *order* our views of evil. This approach contrasts with one which believes we should not involve ourselves with it at all, should not 'put a foot in the devil's door', but just strive for goodness alone. In our day and age, though, we can only do real good when we gain access to an *actual* spiritual knowledge of the powers which wish to lead us astray from a truly human path through all kinds of lures and temptations. Such knowledge makes us aware of what is right and necessary for the human being, helps us take hold of our humanity in freedom.

The science of the spirit transposes questions about the nature of evil from the prison of reason and logic to the free and open ground of life itself. By experiencing the spirit, quite new impulses and tasks arise in our present-day relationship to the issue of evil. Rudolf Steiner never intended to scare-monger with his descriptions of evil's apocalyptic progress (unlike many who take the line that moral preaching is the most effective tool). He wanted, rather, to provide a foundation for knowledge itself to become a morally active deed. Such understanding of evil is therefore not censure, but first and foremost *self-knowledge*.

I must also point out something else of fundamental importance. Our thinking is so ingrained with a dualistic view of the opposition between good and evil (other variations of this dualism can be seen in concepts of heaven and hell, spirit and matter, soul and body, etc.), that we overlook the fact that we cannot usefully solve the riddle of evil in this way. The 'prison' of dialectical reasoning only lets us, as it were, pace from one side of the cell to the other. An example of this is embodied in the assumption that there is only *one* negative opposite to courage. In fact there are two: cowardice on the one hand, extreme daredevil exploits on the other. Evil or wrong always has *two* aspects or extremes, which, it is true, are in stark contrast to one another. We must overcome dualism if we are to have any chance of solving first the philosophical problem of evil and then its reality in our lives; and we can do this by recognizing that it can manifest in one of two contrary forms, and that good is therefore a question of mediation and balance. This is why it is so hard to grasp. Let us look at another example: our health. To say that this is the opposite of illness is empty and abstract. But when we realize that the

body is continually exposed to two opposing tendencies—cooling and hardening on the one hand, and inflammatory and dissolving on the other—health becomes a real concept. It can then be seen to consist of a harmonious balance, an equilibrium between polar opposites, and is therefore no longer just a static condition but a *process*. If dualism was a true perspective on the human being, our inbreathing and outbreathing would have to be seen in terms of good and evil (or vice versa)—obviously a crazy notion! Human life, like all life, unfolds in the tension between polarities. In the same way our greatest good—freedom—develops in the space we create between opposite extremes (such as uncontrolled drives and urges on the one hand, and abstract moral principles on the other), each of which represents an infringement of our humanity. If this were not so, we would be forced into the cleft-stick of judging a sexual offender or someone who had done something criminal from total lack of self-control to have acted in an evil way, while an Adolf Eichmann, a model of 'selfless obedience' and 'duty', would have to be called good. We experience our highest degree of freedom not in a choice between one of two options, a good and a bad, as Kant believed, but in finding a balance. This stands upon its head a widespread theological view of the relationship between freedom and evil. Evil is not the result of the freedom we gained at the Fall, of our intentional divergence from the will of divine powers; true freedom will, rather, only gradually develop through the painful experience of our imperfections which make us a source of evil. It may seem paradoxical to some, perhaps even blasphemous, but the *mission* of evil is to educate us to freedom. In its fire will be forged the full power of the ego, which develops in the face of obstacle and hindrance. Many people may find this an alarming idea, might prefer to regard freedom as a gift of the 'gods above' and evil as the rubbish and waste which is just 'in the way', spoiling the beauty of Creation. Of course it is far easier to look upon our humanity in terms of a dualistic 'goodness' versus 'evil', than

to see it as an ongoing striving to find a middle position between extremes.

These are, broadly, the themes which this selection of lectures addresses: this book follows a path which passes first through the dualistic opposition of good and evil, selfishness and selflessness, *growth and decay*. At this initial stage, we can examine the source and origins of what we call evil. We can peel away the outer shell to reach the core, the *primal phenomenon* from which evil arises. This is connected with the fact that we are *separated* or distinct ego beings, and that there are other, higher such beings, described in old Christian traditions as the hierarchies of angels. From primal opposition, the *dual* nature of evil, wrong and all one-sidedness evolves. Rudolf Steiner gives names to the beings who are at the root of each polarity: he calls them *luciferic* and *ahrimanic* beings. His descriptions provide us with an almost endless variety and abundance of their different aspects. Above all we soon realize that these beings are not only active in the evil that manifests through humanity, but also work everywhere as formative forces in the objective phenomena of nature. In this realm, evil and good are not relevant concepts; we have to speak instead of contrasting tendencies that express themselves through the opposing dynamics of hardening and dissolving processes. They have an external and sometimes 'bad' influence on human destiny through natural catastrophes and disasters such as volcanic eruptions and hurricanes. Evil is as it were just a specific form of these luciferic and ahrimanic forces which have their rightful place, are at work in the cosmos. *Illnesses* are another such form, and therefore have a *double* aspect: they bear the imprint of certain ahrimanic or luciferic forces, but are at the same time an expression of the law of destiny or karma, by means of which the particular failings or limitations which an individual developed in previous lives can be balanced and healed in his struggle with an external manifestation of these limitations in the form of a particular illness. In this process he has to try to develop the forces and strength which counteract such one-sidedness.

Learning to perceive the non-material aspect of the phenomena of life—the polarity of sclerotic and desolving, feverish tendencies in illness, for instance—is the basis for a science of the spirit, and is what Rudolf Steiner calls *Goetheanism*. Understanding the laws of life helps us begin to solve the riddle of evil. All life is continually evolving, so evil can only be understood in the context of the evolution not only of the human being but also of the whole cosmos. Evil is not a static thing but a *phenomenon of evolution*; it appears, basically, when an organ or a stage of development arises in a temporally or spatially 'dislocated' fashion—at the wrong time or place, either too soon or too late.

Dualism is a real phenomenon of the non-human external world which is everywhere composed of opposites. But we cannot *find ourselves* in such dualism; our real humanity consists in the fact that we come between these opposites, separating or uniting them. To get to grips with the problem of evil we need to see the *trinity* of the human being's position between luciferic and ahrimanic forces.

This brings us to the state of humanity today: we are in danger of being crushed between the pincers of a whole range of dualities—political, religious, ethnic, etc. On the other hand, and in total contrast, we can also see that polar opposite tendencies in the human being are melting down and becoming fused together without any mediating, central realm. A prime manifestation of this is the fusing of an ice-cold power of logic and reason with the erupting volcano of passions and drives. We can see two aspects of such a phenomenon: on the one hand an intensifying, self-realizing egohood, and on the other its reverse, the intensified evil which surrounds us on all sides (and which we also create ourselves). Our increasing consciousness of self is not by itself evil; it all depends on how the ego handles the forces available to it. A heightened capacity for evil is increasingly making itself felt, and this is the shadow-side of that inmost core of self-awareness which Rudolf Steiner termed the development of the *consciousness soul.* There are two possible paths this development can pursue. We can continue to go down the road of *separation*: from our fellow men, from nature, from the spiritual nature of the whole cosmos—which has already been denied. We can't reject the reality of nature, perhaps, but we are in the process of trying to replace it with technology. Or, alternatively—and this requires enormous efforts—we can begin to broaden our separated consciousness so that it once more encompasses everything which we had to forego in the course of evolution in order to attain freedom. The first path will involve head-on collisions between conflicting egotisms, will unleash forces of hatred and destruction to an ever-increasing extent. There is no doubt that this is already happening. The beings who are active in such conflict belong, according to Rudolf Steiner, to a third group of 'adversaries' called *Asuras* in theosophical circles, and 'spirits of egotism' or 'spirits of darkness' in anthroposophical terms. A Goethean view of the Asuras is that they are an intensification and permeation of the luciferic-ahrimanic polarity. This law of intensification of a polarity to a higher, combined permutation, can also be seen at work in the realm of organic nature. There is, then, also a *trinity* of evil which develops through the course of history and evolution.

The two paths before humanity's ego-evolution are expressed in the deep images of the *Apocalypse of St John* as a 'two-edged sword'. The ego is itself this sword. And just as the author of the Apocalypse looked forward into the future, so the science of the spirit can look forward, indeed *it must* do so in regard to the following question: what will come of evil, what will happen to us if we choose the first path that leads us into greater and greater isolation, self-centred egotism, denial of the spirit; and what will happen to us if as a result we are alienated more and more from ourselves as beings of spiritual origin, find ourselves in opposition to our own true nature?

The intensifying evil around us must 'flower' to its full extent; but then its blossoms must die away. This means, though, that it should separate out from evolution, eventually become redundant. But we cannot stand back and hope that this will happen; it must waken in us a moral impulse to transform ourselves, to turn around the power of our own ego. The process of consolidation of our self-awareness makes it necessary for the time being for us to develop forces of antipathy and 'aggression'. But a perspective into the far future shows us that we also need to develop higher forces of *love*, which will eventually enable us to redeem ourselves from a state of 'sin' and separation, from falling under the sway of evil. Then a still greater good will come about. For there is a further mystery connected with evil which people have lost sight of, but which the science of the spirit can once more illumine: the secret of *sacrifice*. Evolution and development are not possible unless beings sacrifice themselves and so provide the foundation for the further development of other beings. (This does not, of course, mean that one who wishes to develop can demand such a sacrifice of others.) Evolution can never fully ripen, can never attain its highest peak if no attempt is made to redeem the beings who have sacrificed themselves in the process. This requires an intensification to the nth degree of the powers of transformation, so that nothing is lost which can be transformed. This was in fact the aim of *Manichaeism*, which surfaced in early Christianity but was then declared a heresy. For this reason, this selection closes with a lecture taken from the sequence on the *Apocalypse of St John*, which points to the future mission of Manichaeism. For although such a task still lies far ahead in our future evolution, and is one that we can, as yet, scarcely dream of, it is possible nevertheless to start practising something of a Manichaean attitude. We can form a quite different relationship to the world if we replace our wish to destroy all forces and energies we judge to be evil with an impulse for their *transformation*.[4] We can also exercise Manichaean love

towards plants and animals, whose evolution represents a sacrifice. The principle of 'rooting out' evil, or of revenge—so dear to the media, politicians and religious leaders—is one based wholly on dualism, and only creates more evil. The desire to transform rather than to eradicate is truly Christian. The divine does not counteract evil by exerting the full might of its power, but through 'powerless and vulnerable love' (Häring,[5] 1985).

In the fifth and final section of this book, the 'blossom' of evil in which the threefold adversarial influences will unite is described as the 'Beast with Two Horns', whose occult number is '666'. The effect of this being is one of hardening egotism; not of loving the world but of squeezing it to the very last drop to gain as much advantage and enjoyment from it as possible. That is also the path of black magic which is the one this 'Beast' wishes to lead us down. And many people today do indeed have an increasing interest in such forms of 'self-realization'. So although the influence of this being will extend forward into the far-distant, apocalyptic future, its present effect is already very relevant. For the 'Beast' (*Sorath* in Hebrew) is a being that has in the past regularly intervened in the course of history. And we can begin to realize that our present time already shows certain apocalyptic signs.

Michael Kalisch

I. ORIGIN AND NATURE OF EVIL

1. Evil Illumined through the Science of the Spirit

It is an age-old question that we will look at today: the origin of evil in the world. And although many people nowadays will consider it has been amply dealt with, the human soul will not feel satisfied with the answers that have been given but will return again and again to ponder the problem. For this is not after all a theoretical or scientific question, but one we continually encounter in life. Our souls are rooted as much in evil and wrong as in what is good and beneficial.[1]

Whether we unroll, as it were, the whole history of human thinking so that it becomes quite clear to us that this question of evil preoccupied philosophers throughout human evolution, or whether we just study the outstanding thinkers of the nineteenth century and our present time, we will have to conclude that even the greatest minds were stumped, brought up short by this problem. So our aim today is to take as our starting-point the conclusions of this winter's lecture cycle,[2] the results of the science of the spirit, and to see if we can get a little closer to an answer to the riddle which evil presents us with. I intentionally say 'a little closer', for the nature of this particular question should remind us that spiritual science not only opens perspectives to us which are closed to outer science, but also gives us a certain humility. Posing the loftiest questions is easy when starting out on a search for knowledge, but we may, even after prolonged and genuine striving, only manage to take the first few tentative steps, perhaps only catch a glimpse of the path which can gradually lead us towards an answer.

Allow me to start by trying to show how deeply this question affected the hearts and souls of important thinkers through the ages. I could go a very long way back; but for the time being let us look at those philosophers from the centuries before Christianity was founded in Greece, the *Stoics*,[3] that remarkable group of thinkers who based their views on the teachings of Socrates and Plato. They tried to discover how someone should behave who wishes to live in a way which corresponds to his inmost being, to the destiny which is his and which he affirms. This was the fundamental question that the Stoics pondered; and the answer, the image, that dawned upon them as an ideal for such a person was that of the Wise Man. It would lead us too far to go into detail about the precise nature of this ideal and how it was connected with the outlook of the Stoics. But keep in mind their perception that the aim of human evolution was to increasingly unfold and develop as self-aware ego-beings, that it was the task of humanity to work towards this state. A Stoic philosopher believed that the ego which enabled the human being to enter into the world with full clarity could be clouded or numbed, and that this happened when someone allowed his emotions to work too strongly into the subtle interplay and fabric of his capacity for picturing and sensing. The Stoic thought that allowing the clarity of one's ego to be overwhelmed, to be muddied by passion and emotion, was a kind of spiritual impotence, and that therefore one should subdue passion and emotion in the human breast and strive for peace and equilibrium.

It is apparent, then, that the Stoics had some inkling of the first steps, such as have often been described here, of the path to a perception of the world of spirit, steps which depend on subduing the wild tempests of passion and emotion which otherwise cloud and weaken the spirit. They were aware that only then can clarity of soul and powers of perception coalesce out of the whole realm of soul experience. It was particularly this aspect of Stoicism, rather overlooked in most studies of the history of philosophy, that I wanted to emphasize in the new edition of my book, *The Riddles of Philosophy*.[4] The Stoics' ideal of the Wise Man embodied this capacity for conquering and subduing passions and emotions. And the person who develops this kind of wisdom and so unites himself with cosmic evolution perceives, as the Stoics perceived, that this evolution has the capacity to make him part of itself, so that his own wisdom mingles with and is subsumed by the flowing streams of cosmic wisdom.

So whenever people ask themselves how the human self can be integrated into the whole structure and fabric of the universe, another question also arises: how can the evil that is active in the breadths of the cosmos and that can oppose human striving for wisdom be compatible with the cosmic wisdom which the human being must assume to exist if he is to submerse himself in it?

The Stoic had an inner perception of what was later called divine providence. So how did he combine these two opposing aspects of evil and wisdom? He viewed this problem in a way similar to people today who do not want to enter fully into the science of the spirit, but who as it were stop at the threshold and find a justification for the existence of evil in the necessity of human freedom. He believed that since people should be *free* to strive towards the ideal of the Wise Man, they should also have the possibility of *not* striving towards it—of submerging themselves instead in passion and emotion. The Stoic believed that in that case people descended into a realm lower than the one they really belonged to; and that it made no more sense to blame cosmic wisdom for this descent than to blame it for the fact that there exist animal, plant and mineral kingdoms beneath the human realm. The Stoics knew there is a realm in which the human being can be submerged, in which his wisdom is lost, but that to ascend from it must be his own free choice and the activity of his own wisdom.

We can see, then, that many of the answers about the meaning of evil which have not penetrated further than the threshold of the science of the spirit were already contained in the ancient wisdom of the Stoics. Subsequent centuries have not really progressed significantly beyond this view. This can become immediately clear to us if we take a look at *St Augustine*,[5] a figure of otherwise great importance who lived in the time that followed the founding of Christianity and had a great influence on western Christianity. He pondered the significance of evil in the world and came to the strange conclusion that evil and wrong actually did not exist at all but were just negations or absence of good. He believed that a finite being has weaknesses and can therefore not continually and everlastingly do good deeds. As a result of this failure, good is inevitably circumscribed and limited and positive good is then absent, rather as shadow can be seen as an absence of light, and called forth by it. Today we may consider such a view rather naive—our thinking has had several centuries to advance since then. Yet a scholar recently provided the very same answer to the same problem: *Campbell*,[6] author of a book called *The New Theology*, whose writings have been very well received in certain circles. He too believes that it is pointless to try to investigate the phenomenon of evil since it does not exist in its own right but only as a simple negative. It is not my aim to go in for hair-splitting, philosophical refutation of the Augustinian-Campbellian point of view. Anyone with unprejudiced common sense will see that the idea of evil as mere absence is no different from the idea of coldness as absence of warmth. Yet if we didn't put on a warm overcoat in cold weather, we would soon have a positively real experience of this negative quality, this absence! This idea, which even great philosophers of the nineteenth century subscribed to, of evil as nothing more than a 'non-positivity', really gets us nowhere.

One could also mention a whole group of other thinkers who developed in a way that came close to the findings of the science of the spirit. One such was *Plotinus*,[7] the neo-Platonist, living in the period after Christ. But there were also many others who pondered the nature of evil and wrong in the world, and saw it in terms of the combined physical and spiritual composition of the human being: by immersing himself in the physical body the human being involves himself in matter, which by its very nature hinders and obstructs the workings of the spirit. They saw this immersion of the spirit in matter as the source of evil both in human life and in the outer world.

But such a view was not one that simply resided in the heads of a few isolated thinkers as a satisfactory solution to the great question of evil in the world. That it is a very widespread concept can become clear if we look at an important thinker from a quite different region: the Japanese philosopher *Nakae Toju,*[8] who was a pupil of the Chinese thinker Wang Yang-Ming and lived in the first half of the seventeenth century. He sees everything which we encounter in the world in terms of duality, of two natures. The one, *Ri,* he looks up to as a realm of spirit in which the human soul participates; the other, *Ki,* is of a physical nature, in which all that is bodily and material has a share. From the combination of Ri and Ki he believes that all beings arise, and that human beings have both aspects. Because the human soul with its Ri-aspect has to immerse itself in the Ki, human will arises; and with will comes desire. So the soul becomes entangled in willing and desiring and develops the potential for evil. This eastern thinker, clearly, is on very similar ground to the western schools of thought expressed by such thinkers as Plotinus: evil as entanglement in matter. This view is actually widespread throughout the broadest circles of human thinking, and we will see later that it is important to be aware of its ramifications.

I would also briefly like to describe the ideas of another thinker, a very important one indeed, *Hermann Lotze,* who lived in the nineteenth century and concerned himself with the origin and nature of evil. His books include various important philosophical works, such as the outstanding *Mikrokosmos* (Microcosm).[9] He was a philosopher in whom heart-forces were particularly developed; he believed that the reality of evil in the world and in ourselves cannot be denied, but rejected the idea of its necessity to our evolution and education. This latter view held that evil and wickedness had to be a part of life for otherwise the human soul would not have any means of purifying and developing itself, no counter-force to oppose so as to educate itself. Lotze was not an atheist but assumed the existence of God as a divine force permeating and imbuing the world. So he questioned these views in the following terms: if we assume that God needed evil and wickedness to enable us to develop and gain freedom of soul, this could only happen through our own inner work, through having our own inner experience of developing and distancing ourselves from evil, so that we could eventually become self-aware, conscious of our true being and worth. But, he said, what about the animal kingdom, in which we see evil and wrong manifest in many ways? In the animal kingdom we can find all sorts of acts of cruelty, which if they enter human life become the most dreadful depravity and vice. But education cannot be cited as a real possibility for the animal kingdom—one cannot re-educate animals' instincts. So Lotze rejected this idea. In particular he drew attention to the fact that the 'education' view contradicted the idea of God's omnipotence; for it would only be necessary to develop from a worse to a better condition if the worse was already originally present—rather an indictment, it seemed to him, of God's Creation.

Instead, Lotze wondered whether it might be more valid to assume, like certain other thinkers, not that evil, wrong and wickedness are present as a result of the conscious will and power of God, but that they are simply 'given': that they are connected with the world in the same way that three angles adding up to 180° is connected with a triangle. Any world which God wished to create would in this version have to be based on what was already a reality independent of him. Evil and wrong as constituent parts of the universal fabric would have to be inherent in God's Creation. But Lotze also rejected this idea. It was, he felt, an even more drastic curtailment of the workings of the divine. For if we look carefully at the world and its laws and phenomena, it would actually seem quite possible to imagine a world without evil. Evil, which infringes our real freedom, must he thought be caused by the free, arbitrary intention of the divine.

I could pursue this train of thought, which Lotze and other thinkers (I have only cited Lotze as one example and type of philosopher) developed in response to the problem of evil. But it is the conclusion which Lotze came to that is important for us. He rejects the German philosopher *Leibniz*, who had written a 'theodicy', a justification of the presence of evil in God's plan, and who adopted the view that this was the 'best of all possible worlds', even though much evil exists. Leibniz said that if this was not the best possible world, then God must either not have known anything better—which violates the idea of his omniscience; or he must have not wanted to create a better—which is a breach of his all-graciousness; or he must have been unable to create a better—which renders void the idea of his omnipotence. Since Leibniz believed that our thinking cannot accept that these three principal qualities of God can be violated, he assumed that this must be the best possible world. Lotze countered that it was not possible to speak of God's omnipotence if one attributed evil and wrong to a divine source, and that therefore Leibniz had only salvaged for himself this teaching of our world being the best possible by limiting God's omnipotence.

Lotze thought that there was a way out of this impasse: in the broad span of the cosmos he believed that order and harmony reigned and that evil was only apparent in particular and specific details. What does it mean, wondered Lotze, if this is the case, if the whole universe is actually ordered and harmonious, yet evil and wrong appear everywhere like black specks in specific, individual contexts? His conclusion was that the existence of both evil and good must be due to a divine wisdom that we cannot fathom. Therefore we must accept that the problem of evil represents a threshold to our powers of perception beyond which we cannot go. There must in this view be a wisdom beyond human wisdom and understanding, which has a use and justification for evil. Lotze therefore transposes understanding of evil and wrong into an unknown, inaccessible world of wisdom.

This may all appear rather pedantic and convoluted to many, but I wanted to show what cudgels philosophers have taken up to beat a path towards understanding evil, and how puny and unsuitable these weapons have actually proved in the attempt to solve a riddle which we are faced with at every turn of our daily lives.

There are other thinkers as well who tried to get a bit further than Plotinus by tapping into the deep sources of existence—which can actually only be done by developing the soul to a higher capacity of perception. Such a thinker was *Jacob Boehme*.[10] Few people now wish to study his ideas, formulated in the sixteenth-seventeenth centuries, though he is considered something of an interesting curiosity. Boehme tried to penetrate the depths of the world and its phenomena to the extent of feeling a kind of theosophy, a kind of divinity dawn within his soul. At the same time he tried to find ways of tracing evil and wrong back to a source in the deep underground springs of the world, of sensing that they are not just something negative but rooted in the very fabric of the world and our humanity. Boehme sees divine being as something within which 'differentiation'* must arise—you have to get used to his way of expressing things. A being, he thought, which simply allows its activity to stream out into the world, could never manage to become aware of itself. This activity has to encounter some opposition, come up against something else. A small example of this occurs every morning when we wake up: we are then to some degree capable of unfolding our soul and spirit activity out of the unbounded depths of our soul and spirit; at that point our soul-spirit comes up against our surroundings, which makes us aware of ourselves once

* German: *Schiedlichkeit*.

more. We actually only become aware of ourselves in the physical world by encountering the opposition of things around us. Divine being cannot encounter such opposition from other beings. It has to be its own adversary, or as Boehme puts it, set its own 'yes' against its own 'no'. It has to set boundaries within itself to its infinite, out-streaming activity. It must become 'differentiated', must, at some point of its sphere of activity, create its own opposite in order to become self-aware. Boehme believed, then, that it was not so much through the outpourings of divine being that all evil and wrong arises, but through the beings which the divine must create as its necessary adversaries. It is therefore not right to speak of evil and wrong so much as of the conditions necessary for the divine to perceive itself. The creations and 'creatures' which do not embed themselves in the out-streaming life of the divine, but form an adversarial hindrance, give rise to evil and wrong.

Such an answer to the problem will certainly not satisfy anyone who tries to penetrate the secrets of existence through the science of the spirit. I have only mentioned it here to show you some of the profounder depths an acute thinker can plumb when trying to discover the source of evil in the world. I could cite many other ways in which people have tried to approach this riddle, without however being able to seek confirmation of their ideas in the reality of the world itself.

Lotze, this very acute thinker of the nineteenth century, believes that there must exist a wisdom which somehow justifies evil and wrong. But our capacity for knowledge is circumscribed and limited—according to him we cannot penetrate this wisdom. This surely is yet another example of a particular preconception of our time: the belief that we should just accept as they are our human capacities for knowledge and understanding, not bothering to imagine that it might be possible for them to develop beyond their normal, ordinary functions and allow us to perceive and penetrate other worlds than the realm of the senses and sense-bound reason. It is surely not too far-fetched to think that important questions, such as that about the origin of evil, have not been able to be answered for the very reason that people were so reluctant to go beyond the kinds of knowledge and perception which depend upon these senses and this sense-bound reason; and so were unable to attain a different sort of knowledge—one that has been described here on many occasions, one through which the human soul develops beyond its ordinary, everyday ways of perceiving, and its normal scientific outlook.

We have often spoken of the human soul's potential for working its way free from the physical body, for accomplishing that spiritual chemistry in which, just as hydrogen separates out from water, the soul and spirit separates out from the body. When this happens, when the human being lifts himself up into the realm of spirit so that as a being of soul and spirit he stands separate from and outside his body and can perceive a world of spirit, then he can begin to have immediate, direct, body-free experience of the deep, underlying fabric of the world.

It is perhaps legitimate to ask what results we are likely to obtain if we really try to pursue this path of spiritual research—which I have frequently described and which is presented in detail in my book *Knowledge of the Higher Worlds.* Of particular interest to us today is the way in which what we normally call evil relates to this path. When the spiritual researcher elevates himself to higher worlds, separates out his soul and spirit from the body in order to perceive in a body-free state, then all that he looks back on and recognizes as evil, or even only incomplete in his life, provides the greatest obstacle and hindrance to his path of development. The greatest obstacles are formed by those aspects which he looks back on and sees are unfinished or imperfect. I certainly don't wish to sound arrogant by suggesting that only perfect people can develop the capacity to perceive the spiritual world. All I am saying is that the path to spiritual perception involves a certain kind of martyrdom; for the moment we separate out our soul and spirit from the body and begin to be participators in the world of spirit, we look back on our life with all its imperfections and realize that these follow us like the tail follows the comet. We realize that we must carry them on with us into other lives, will have to try to resolve them, balance them out in the future; that all we blithely ignored previously and were as unaware of as the ground under our feet, now lies clearly before us as an inevitable task we must get to grips with. It is this somewhat tragic realization, this perception of the nature of our ordinary, everyday selves, which hampers us when we try to ascend into the world of spirit. If it does not hamper us, if we do not feel burdened by the more ponderous, earnest aspects of life, we can be sure that we have not found a real path to the spirit. And even if we do not manage to get any further, this one realization is of great value, this infinitely clear and vivid perception of the evil and imperfection within ourselves. So we can see that our very first steps of ascent into the world of spirit are accompanied by an experience of evil and imperfection.

Why is this? If we look closer, we can recognize in this fact a fundamental trait of all human evil. In my last book, *The Threshold of the Spiritual World*, I tried to elaborate on this basic characteristic of the evil emanating from human beings. The common trait of all evil is nothing other than egotism. If I was to try to provide detailed evidence for this I would have to talk on for hours and hours—instead I will just put it to you, and leave it to you to tease out the threads and trains of thought yourselves. I will pick them up again in my next lecture, where I wish to speak of the 'moral basis of human life'.[11] Basically, all human evil proceeds from what we call egotism. In the whole scope and range of 'wrong', from the smallest oversight to the most serious crime, whether the imperfection or evil originates more in the body or in the soul, egotism is the fundamental trait which underlies it all. We can ascertain the real meaning of evil by connecting it in our minds with human egotism, and all striving to reach beyond

imperfection and evil involves a struggle with egotism. Much philosophy has striven to establish ethical principles and moral foundations of one kind or another, but the deeper one penetrates into such principles and foundations, the more one becomes aware that egotism is actually the common factor underlying all human evil, and that the path which leads beyond evil here in the physical world is the one upon which we combat egotism.

Alongside this realization we have to admit another, one which confronts us in our spiritual research as something of a quite distressing nature. For when we examine the faculties and capacities we need to develop in order to elevate ourselves into the worlds of spirit, into the worlds we can only perceive in a body-free state, when we consider the soul-exercises which must be practised to ascend into these worlds,[12] we find that quite particular qualities and characteristics must be strengthened in the soul. These are ones which in the sense-world make the soul stronger, more independent and self-reliant. Qualities in other words which in the physical sense-world appear as egotism, must actually be strengthened and intensified to enable us to ascend into the world of spirit. Only when the soul has developed this self-rooted ego-strength can it begin to rise up into higher worlds of spirit. We are therefore confronted by an apparent paradox: that the qualities which infringe the moral principles we would wish to adopt in the physical world, are precisely the ones we need to reinforce and strengthen on the path to perception of the worlds of spirit.

An important mystic has said:

When the rose adorns itself.
It also adorns the garden.[13]

This is no doubt true within certain bounds. But in ordinary human life it would be egotistic for the soul to view itself only as a self-adorning rose. The saying, though, is absolutely true of conditions in the world of spirit, where the more a soul has strengthened itself and developed the inner wealth of its potential, the more it can participate and serve the whole. Just as we cannot really make anything worthwhile with imperfect tools, so the soul cannot make much use of itself until it has drawn out from the ego what is inherent in itself.

So we can start to go beyond clever phrases and see the real state of affairs, observing that the world of spirit and that of the physical senses are mutually interrelated, that the latter must fulfil its obligation towards the former. If we lived in the world of spirit alone, we would only be able to develop inner capacities of self, as expressed in that saying: 'When the rose adorns itself, it also adorns the garden'. But we could not develop the capacity for altruism which enables us to unite with other people, with the whole world. Only in the physical world can we find conditions which allow us to overcome egotism. In these conditions it is altruism we need to develop, in order to 'break the habit' of egotism as thoroughly as possible.

The same principle which is decisive for the spiritual researcher, the strengthening of soul which allows him to elevate himself to the world of spirit, is equally decisive when we die and enter the realm in which we remain between death and a new birth. We then become part of that same world which the spiritual researcher gains access to through developing certain capacities of soul. Into these conditions we need to bring the inner strength of our soul, the qualities expressed in the saying: 'When the rose adorns itself, it also adorns the garden'. The moment we pass through the threshold of death we enter a realm in which the intensification and strengthening of our ego is the important thing. I will speak more of that in the lecture 'Between Death and Rebirth'.[14] But for now I only want to point out that the soul in the spiritual world between death and rebirth is primarily concerned with itself, with its own destiny resulting from previous earthly lives.

The human soul, then, appears to us in a dual aspect: inhabiting this great 'school' of earthly conditions it must learn to grow out of and beyond itself, so that egotism can transmute into altruism and so that the soul can be of significance and worth for the wide world of which it is a part. But into the realm between death and new birth, in contrast, the soul must bring inner strength, for there, otherwise, it has nothing to offer.

What does this dual nature of the soul actually mean for us?

It means that we must be very careful not to falsely transpose something that has its rightful place in one world—the intensification of inner strength in the world of spirit—to another, the physical world, except when we are attempting to penetrate the world of spirit. It means that only evil will come of the human being allowing his *earthly sense-nature* to be permeated by this inner intensification and self-consolidation, even though this *is* exactly what the realm of spirit requires. The strengthening and empowering of our ego in the world of spirit between death and new birth is actually what enables us to prepare an incarnation in the physical sense-world in which our outer actions and thoughts can become as unegotistic as possible. We need to use our egotism before birth in the world of spirit to work upon ourselves, to look at ourselves in such a way that subsequently in the physical world we can become more selfless and unselfish—moral, in other words.

This is really the nub of the matter for anyone who wants to penetrate into the world of spirit. We have to be clear that there is a good reason why, in the world of spirit, we perceive all that is evil and imperfect in us as a shadow-image. This is what shows us that we must remain connected to the sense-world, that our karma, our destiny, must continue to bind us to the sense-world until we finally reach the stage of being united in spirit with the whole world, rather than living in our own small realm of self-concern. It shows us that what is absolutely necessary for spiritual progress, perfecting and intensifying one's own being, is a source of evil and wrong if transposed directly upon the things of outer, physical life. Making spiritual progress, though, is not something we should allow ourselves to be deterred from. It is, rather, our duty to pursue it. Evolution, which for all other living creatures is a law of nature, is for us a duty and task. Nevertheless it is wrong to apply directly to outer life the striving which is right for spiritual evolution. Outer physical life and the morality appropriate to it are a distinct realm, a second world alongside the world of spirit which the soul strives inwardly to attain.

But now we are faced with something of a paradox—although such living contradictions are, one might say, the very fabric of the world. I have said that we need to strengthen ourselves inwardly; the ego, the I, must become stronger in order to penetrate into the spiritual world. Yet if we only developed egotism in our spiritual ascent we would not get very far. What does this mean? We must penetrate the world of spirit without egotism, yet we *cannot* penetrate it without egotism (a fact that everyone must sadly acknowledge who enters the spiritual world). What this means is that we must have our egotism before us, be aware of it in such an objective way that we can see it, recognize it as the egotism we are bound up with in the outer world. In other words we must strive to become unegotistic with the means at our disposal in physical, earthly life, for when we reach the spiritual world we no longer have the opportunity to become selfless, since there we must unfold and strengthen the inner powers of the soul. That is the—only apparent—contradiction. Whether we enter the spiritual world through self-development or by passing over the threshold of death, we must dwell there within the inner strength of our being. Yet we cannot manage this unless we develop altruism in the physical world. Altruism in the physical world has its mirror-image in the rightful egotism needed in the world of spirit.

So you can see how difficult the concepts become when we come closer to the spiritual world. But this perspective also starts to shed light on earthly, human life. Let us imagine for instance a person entering physical existence, being born, who clothes the being which he was between a previous death and his present birth in a physical body. It can happen that he wrongly imbues his physical body with what we might call the vital energy of the world of spirit, that the spirit becomes confused in the physical situation and transposes into the earthly realm the quality that has its rightful place in the spiritual. In such an instance good becomes evil! This is a most important secret of existence—that the quality integral to our spiritual being, one that represents our highest attainment in the world of spirit, can be wrongly transposed and relocated in the physical realm, so that it becomes our worst aberration.

So we can begin to answer the question about the origin of evil and wrong-doing in the world. It comes about when we allow our better, higher nature (*not* our worst) to descend and be submerged in the physical realm, a realm which cannot as such be evil. It comes about when we develop qualities in the physical realm which do not belong there, which have their rightful place in the realm of spirit. Why do we have a potential for evil? Because we are also spiritual beings! Because we have to be able to develop those qualities when we penetrate into the spiritual world, which become bad when we apply them in the physical. Qualities which manifest as cruelty or malice in the physical world, if withdrawn from the physical realm and allowed instead to imbue the inwardness of the soul, to unfold in the world of spirit, become qualities which advance and perfect us. What brings about evil is misapplying spiritual qualities to physical life. If we could not be evil, we could not be spiritual beings either. Without the characteristics which make us evil, we could not enter the spiritual world.

Perfection consists in learning to imbue our inner being with the recognition that we should not transpose qualities to the physical realm which make us evil. For the more we wrongly draw such qualities down into the physical, then the more we also deprive our inner soul of these qualities, weaken our connection with the spiritual world, where such qualities actually belong.

The science of the spirit can help us to see that evil and wrong demonstrate the existence of a soul-spirit world alongside the physical. Why else does a thinker like Lotze stop short, rein in his investigations of evil in the physical world? It is because his powers of perception are not prepared to penetrate into the spiritual world, and that evil cannot be explained in physical terms since it is in fact a misuse of forces which belong to the world of spirit! It is therefore no wonder that philosophers who disregard a world of spirit are unable to trace the origin of evil in the physical sense-world.

But when we turn our attention to other kinds of wrong or evil that are not connected with human beings—which we can recognize for instance in the animal kingdom—we find that we are not the only beings to wrongly transpose qualities which have their rightful place in the world of spirit. The animal kingdom can show us that there are spiritual beings which create evil in a realm where the human being cannot. In other words, when we try to discover the source of evil in the world, we recognize that it is not only ourselves who introduce imperfections into physical existence. So we can start to understand what is meant when a spiritual researcher says the animal kingdom is basically the manifestation of an invisible world of spirit, in which beings, prior to the human being, did the same as the human being now does—wrongfully transposing the spirit into the physical world. This is the cause and origin of all that we may recognize as cruel or wrong in the animal kingdom. I would like to emphasize that those who believe that evil can be ascribed to the entanglement of our soul in the material world are mistaken. It is important to realize that the spiritual qualities and capacities of the human being are the source of evil. And that there would be little wisdom in a cosmic order which so circumscribed the human being that he could only give rise to goodness, not evil, in the sense-world; in an order which as we have seen would have to rob him of the forces which he needs to advance and ascend into the spiritual world. We are beings who simultaneously belong to both physical and spiritual worlds, in whom the spiritual law not of imperfection but of perfection is at work. As such we are capable of gravitating more in one direction or another, of swinging like a pendulum as far back as we have swung forward; are capable because we are spirit beings of bearing spirit into the physical world and embodying it as evil, just as other, perhaps higher, beings are capable of embodying evil by transposing into the sense-world what should belong only to the world of spirit.

I realize that such a perspective on the source of evil is one which few people perhaps will be able to relate to, but which nevertheless will increasingly root itself in the life of the human soul. People will increasingly find that problems in the world can only be dealt with when they begin to conceive of another, spiritual world underpinning it. They may perhaps, though this too is an illusion, live quite easily with the perfections of the physical sense-world; but the imperfection, the evil and wrong, will be beyond them unless they grow capable of seeing its origin in a dislocation of those spiritual qualities which help them advance when applied to their proper, spiritual realm.

I'm sure I don't need to state that it would be utter nonsense to conclude from what I have said that only rascals and criminals can make progress in the spiritual world. That would be a complete misreading of the truth. It would be like accusing me of saying that it is good for a person to have the strength to smash a clock to pieces. Of course it is good to have such strength, but it does not need to be used in that way. It can equally well be used for a useful, helpful purpose, and is then a force for good not evil. To realize that it is the misapplication of the powers and forces we need to perfect ourselves that causes evil can give us a deep insight into the mysteries of human existence.

In our present time, we can be aware that a decided impetus

and inclination towards the worlds of spirit is arising in the deep regions of the soul. This fact can help us to a clearer and more detailed understanding of the period leading from the nineteenth century to the present day. In the nineteenth century, the school of *Pessimism* gathered a certain momentum among philosophers. They looked at evil in the world and concluded, some of them at least—such as *Schopenhauer*[15] and *Eduard von Hartmann*[16]—that we should not regard the world as a place which wants anything other from the human being than his demise. They believed that the only possible salvation for the individual is to be re-absorbed into the natural processes of the world, rather than to strive towards a goal which affords personal fulfilment of any kind. I am not so interested in this conclusion itself as in what underlies it: the fact that the soul was imprisoned during the age of materialism, that absolutely no comfort could be found to redress the balance of evil and wrong in the world, since materialism rejects the idea of a world of spirit. Yet it is this world alone which can illuminate the meaning of evil.

Rather than speaking of Nietzsche today, I will mention another thinker of the nineteenth century, one who appears in something of a tragic light if you consider that people are more or less constrained by the times in which they live. There is characteristically a confluence of our being with the being of the time we inhabit. It was therefore quite natural that particularly those with deep minds and open hearts for the influences around them were powerfully moved by a world-view which tried to explain all life in terms of outer phenomena. But such minds were frequently too perceptive to succumb to the illusion that we can go through life, can observe the evil in the world, without the comfort of a world of spirit which can reconcile us to evil's necessity.

Philipp Mainländer,[17] born in 1841, experienced the tragic aspects of materialism although he himself never became a materialist. Outwardly he was, one can say, a follower of Schopenhauer, but he came to his own unusual and distinct world-view. Although possessing a deep mind he was also a child of his time, and so was capable only of taking into account the things of the material world. This materialism exerted a particularly strong, imprisoning influence, we should be clear, on the best minds and souls of the day. The people who remain unaffected by the spirit of their time, who wrap their religious confession comfortably around them—the most 'religious' people—are sometimes the most egotistic in this respect. They reject anything which goes beyond the narrow confines of what is safe and familiar to them. Frequently when I draw attention to the tragedy of countless souls imprisoned in a materialistic outlook, people suggest that a good, old-fashioned form of Christianity would do such souls more good than my new-fangled science of the spirit. But such a suggestion only shows that they are not properly part of their own times, shows an intolerance towards the new impetus which strives to penetrate our cultural evolution for the good of humanity.

Philipp Mainländer surveyed all that outer science and the materialism of our time had to offer, and could find only a world and a humanity characterized by evil. He could not find a real way through the soul-constricting fetters of this materialism so as to be able to look up towards a world of spirit. And why is it indeed, let us ask ourselves, that so few people find their way to the science of the spirit? The pressure of preconception and prejudice exerted by materialism, or the more refined name it is known by nowadays, Monism, is so strong that it clouds and darkens the vision of our souls for the spiritual world. If people were left to themselves, not swayed and pressurized by such an outlook, they would doubtless find their way to the science of the spirit. But the pressure has been very great, and only now at last, in our present time, has an era begun to dawn in which we can have some hope that people will be open to hearing about the science of the spirit. Their longing has become so urgent that this science of the spirit must find an echo in their souls. In the last two-thirds of the nineteenth century there was little chance of such an echo. The pressure of materialism was then so strong that even someone whose soul longed for the spirit, like Philipp Mainländer, was held back. He was bowed under the force of this general outlook and could come only to the belief that the world as it stood before him was devoid of spirit. Mainländer exerted no great influence on his contemporaries, but this was only because the spirit of the age, in spite of all its material advances, was fundamentally shallow. But Mainländer still felt what every soul had to feel somewhere in its depths in the nineteenth century. He was a man of wisdom and integrity compared with those whose spirits were clouded and weakened and who therefore disregarded all that was left unsatisfied by a materialistic or Monistic outlook. Rather than ploughing through the weighty volumes of his *Philosophy of Redemption*, you can understand his views by referring to the excellent little booklet by Max Seiling.[18]

Philipp Mainländer inevitably saw the world as it appeared to his senses and reason, bowed down as he was by the force of materialism. But he was not satisfied. He needed to posit a world of spirit; yet this, he said to himself, did not exist, and therefore the sense-world must be explained only in terms of itself. The conclusion he worked his way through to was that there had been a world of spirit which preceded ours, that our soul had previously dwelt in a divine and spiritual realm from which we had passed into our present form of existence; that our present world could only exist because God and the spiritual world had died away before us. So he came to the idea of a world of spirit, but not one which still existed within our world. Our world he saw as a kind of corpse burdened with evil, whose only further function was to be assigned to oblivion, so that whatever had led to the demise of God and the world of spirit could also finally be destroyed. Monists or other thinkers may chuckle at such ideas. But whoever has some insight into the way a soul may be imbued with a particular general outlook to the extent that it becomes inner destiny can understand what Mainländer must have gone through in being compelled to transpose the spiritual world to a dead past, and to see the present world as nothing but the corpse of the divine. Mainländer was driven to this conclusion in his attempt to understand the evils of the world. We can see that his views went inwardly deeper than those of, say, Nietzsche or Schopenhauer, or Bahnsen[19]—or Eduard von Hartmann. At the age of 35, when he had completed his *Philosophy of Redemption*, he felt that he now needed to shed the body, that his strength would be more available for helping to further humanity's redemption in a bodiless form than if he continued to inhabit his body past the mid-point of life. We can see the deep seriousness and inner consistency of his conclusions, compared with Schopenhauer and the others, in the fact that he pursued his convictions to the uttermost extreme; that because he felt he should pour out his strength into the world rather than concentrate it within his body, he killed himself.

Philosophers and others may like to ignore such a destiny, but it is of fundamental importance for our times, showing as it does what the soul must undergo if it really penetrates to the longing in its depths, and if it is faced with the problem of evil without any vision of the world which radiates spiritual light and illumines evil's purpose and meaning. It was necessary for the human soul to evolve materialistic capacities. At some point in the future, people will view the life of the spirit in terms of a 'psycho-biology', in terms of the soul, and realize that what we find as a physical reflection, in the animal kingdom for example, also applies to the human being, but only when elevated to the realm of spirit. Certain kinds of animal can go without food for long periods of time. Tadpoles, for instance, can be induced to turn more quickly into frogs by letting them go hungry. Similar processes can be found in certain fish which sometimes do not eat for a long period: this initiates transformations which allow them to carry out whatever it is they need to. They go hungry so that the forces which are otherwise involved in feeding and digestion can be redirected to form new structures. This is an image which we can apply to the human soul: for centuries it has lived through a period in which the belief held sway that there are limits to human knowledge, and even today there are many who are still deeply imbued with materialistic concepts—though people now prefer to call them Monistic because they feel a little ashamed of them—even though they consider their thoughts to be spiritual. The capacities which led us to this point had to evolve. In other words humanity had to pass through a period of spiritual starvation, the era of materialism. But the forces which were thereby held back in the soul can now, in accordance with a psycho-biological law, lead the human soul to seek the worlds of spirit. People will even discover that human discontent at being unable to find the world of spirit in the physical world actually could have taken no other form than that demonstrated by Mainländer. Materialism robbed him of the spiritual world, and so he felt helpless in the face of the physical; his only mistake was not to perceive that the world which he thought had preceded the physical 'corpse' gives us the possibility of finding something within our souls which leads us towards the future, as certainly as the external world points back to the past. In a certain respect, Mainländer was absolutely correct: the world around us represents the remains of a previous evolutionary process. Even modern geologists have to admit that this earth we walk upon is a corpse. But what Mainländer failed to see is that as we walk upon this corpse we simultaneously develop a seed for the future within us. When we survey the meaning of the science of the spirit for each individual soul, something can flare up in us which Mainländer could not yet perceive, and so despaired.

We stand at the knife-edge between two epochs: that of materialism and that of the science of the spirit. And there is perhaps—if we truly understand our own soul—nothing which can better prove to us the need to work and live towards a future age of spirituality than examining the question of evil, so long as we can also turn our gaze upwards to the illumined heights of the world of spirit. I have often said that we can feel ourselves in harmony in such contemplations with the best minds of all periods, who delved deep to find ways in which humanity should live towards the future. Such a mind was Goethe; and an aphorism he coined about the outer world of the senses, like a trumpet call heralding our need to develop spiritual knowledge, is one which can sum up the things we have spoken of today, and to which we can respond with a transforming echo.

Goethe, in *Faust*, gives us four beautiful lines which show how human beings have distanced themselves from the spirit:

> He who seeks knowledge of living things
> First tries to drive out spirit's wings;
> In his hands the separate parts lie dead—
> Unjoined, alas, by spirit's living thread.[20]

It was human destiny to devote several centuries to investigating the separate 'components' of the world. But now, increasingly, people will feel not only the theoretical lack, but also the deep loss, of the missing spiritual 'thread' which unites these components into a living whole. The spiritual researcher can today perceive what most souls are still unaware of: their longing for the world of spirit. And our contemplation of the nature of evil can perhaps lead us to broaden the scope of Goethe's lines in a way that encompasses all that we have spoken of today.

Goethe saw that it is not enough to dissect the parts if we are to arrive at a view and vision of the whole and above all at an understanding of the spirit. And after trying to come close to an answer to the riddle of evil, we can go one step further and, drawing on the deep foundations of a science of the spirit, sum up our conviction with the following feeling:

Merely dwelling in the sense-world's light
Will never solve soul's riddle or soul's plight;
The world and life we'll only understand
When to spirit heights we strive, ascend!

2. Good and Evil: Creation and Death

Yesterday we considered the successive moods of soul that have to be attained if human thinking, what we ordinarily think of as knowledge, is to penetrate reality, and we came to a condition of soul which we called 'surrender'—a thinking in other words that has elevated itself first to *wonder*, has then learned what we called *reverent devotion to the world of reality*, and has subsequently progressed to the condition we described as *knowing ourselves to be in wise harmony with the phenomena of the world*. A thinking not capable of rising in this way, so that it enters the realm characterized by humility and surrender, cannot penetrate reality. Such surrender can only be attained by continually endeavouring to remind ourselves of the inadequacy of mere thought. We have to make an energetic effort, take great pains to stimulate and strengthen within us the kind of mood which does not expect our thinking to give us knowledge of the truth, but only to educate us. It is of the utmost importance that we should develop in ourselves this idea of the educative value of thinking. If you really adopt this as a practical rule of life, you will find that you arrive on many occasions at quite different conclusions from those that at first seemed inevitable.

I imagine that only very few of you will have made a thorough study of *Kant's* philosophy.[1] There is no need to do so. I only want to refer to the fact that in Kant's most important and revolutionary work, *The Critique of Pure Reason*, you will find that he always provides proofs both for and against each proposition. Take, for instance, the following statement: 'The world once had a beginning in time'. Opposite this, you will find that Kant places the contradictory assertion: 'The world has always existed'. He then proceeds to offer valid proofs for both statements, in spite of the fact that they are diametrically opposed. He proves, in other words, both that the world had a beginning and that it never had a beginning. This method of reasoning he calls 'antinomy', believing it to show that there are definite boundaries and limitations to the human capacity for knowledge, since we can use reason to arrive at quite contradictory conclusions. And he is right, of course, if we imagine that we can arrive at the truth—become one, in other words, with some objective, ultimate reality—through elaborating concepts, or through applying a process of thinking to our experiences. We are really in something of a plight if we expect to attain truth in this way and are then shown that two quite opposite statements can both be proved correct. But if, instead, we have learned to see that thinking actually does not provide us with a clear-cut sword of judgement in matters of reality, if we have energetically educated ourselves to view thinking as a *means* to become wiser, to pursue our self-education towards wisdom, then we will remain unmoved by the fact that two completely opposing statements can both be proved.

In fact we soon make the following discovery: there is actually a direct connection between the fact that elaborating concepts does not lead us to penetrate reality, and the perfect freedom we can acquire within the sphere of concepts, which allows us to pursue our own self-education. If we were always subject to correction by reality then our elaboration of concepts would not provide us with a free and independent means of self-education. Please think about this carefully. Let me repeat it once more: by elaborating concepts we have an effective and independent means of self-education; and this can only come about because reality never interferes in this free activity.

What does this mean? What sort of interference or disturbance would reality make in the free elaboration of concepts? We can get some idea of this if we contrast—quite hypothetically for now, though later we will see that it does not remain wholly hypothetical—our human thinking with divine thinking. It is surely impossible to imagine that divine thinking could be unconnected with reality. When we try to imagine the thinking of the gods we can only picture it, still speaking hypothetically for the moment, as participating in and influencing reality. The inevitable conclusion we must draw from this is as follows: a human mistake in thinking is a mere logical mistake, nothing worse. If we later realize we have made a mistake, we can correct it, and at the same time we will have learnt something in the process, grown a little wiser. But when divine thinking is correct then something happens or is created; when it thinks falsely something is destroyed, annihilated. If we had a divine form of thinking, each false concept of ours would initiate a destructive process, starting in our astral body and continuing on into our etheric and then physical bodies. If we had active, divine thinking, if our thinking had something to do with reality, then a false concept would stimulate within us a drying-up process in some part or other of our body, a hardening process. In that sort of situation, you will agree, mistakes would not be welcome! We might soon make so many mistakes that our body dried up altogether and fell to pieces. If our mistakes in thinking were transformed into reality, our body would soon be quite worn out. The fact that our thinking does not interfere with reality is what maintains us, allows us to dwell within reality. We can make conceptual mistake after mistake without any harmful consequences. If we later correct these mistakes we have educated ourselves by means of them, have grown wiser, but without inflicting catastrophic consequences on ourselves or our surroundings. When we imbue ourselves more and more with the moral force contained in such an idea as this, we learn to know the nature of the 'surrender' of which I spoke, and we no longer, finally, look upon thinking as something which we can apply at critical moments of life to gain knowledge of outer things.

That sounds strange, I know, and at first sight impossible. How can we stop applying our thinking to external circumstances? We cannot it is true do this in an absolute sense, but we can manage it in certain specific conditions. As human beings in the world, we cannot on every occasion suspend judgement about external matters. We have to judge things and form opinions—we shall see in the course of these lectures why this is so; we have to be active in life, perform deeds which actually do not penetrate the depths of reality. So we have to make decisions and come to conclusions, but we can also exercise caution in accepting as finally true the judgements and opinions we form. We should as it were continually be looking over our own shoulder and reminding ourselves that precisely when we apply our keenest powers of intellect we are treading on very uncertain ground, are likely to continually make mistakes. That is a hard thing for cocksure people to accept! To doubt their own opinion would seem to them nothing but a hindrance. You may have noticed that many people often find it necessary to underline their opinions with such phrases as: 'But what I think is this'; or when they see something, to say: 'I like this', or 'I don't like that'. That is the kind of attitude, though, which must be relinquished by anyone who wants to go deeper and further than an easy self-assurance. It must be given up if we want to set the course of our life in the direction of reality. Instead we need to cultivate a state of mind which can be characterized as follows: although we have to live our life in the world and therefore form opinions, and must use our powers of judgement to make our way through life, we *can* refrain from making ready judgements in the recognition of *truth*. As far as truth itself is concerned, we can adopt an attitude of caution, doubt and scrutiny towards every judgement that we make.

But how, then, are we to arrive at any idea about truth if we do not form judgements in the ordinary way? We discussed yesterday the state of mind necessary for this, describing it as one in which we allow things themselves to speak and tell us  their secrets. We have to learn to adopt a passive attitude to the things we encounter in the world, listen to them in such a way that they begin to tell us their secrets. Many errors and mistakes would be avoided if people would practise this. We have a wonderful example of this in Goethe, who refrained from judging and concluding in his investigations of truth, but instead tried to let the things themselves utter their secrets. Let us imagine that there are two people—one who judges and the other who lets the things themselves reveal their secrets. Let's take a very clear, simple example. One person sees a wolf and describes it. He finds there are other animals which resemble the wolf, and he arrives by a process of deduction at the general concept of 'wolf'. And now he can go on to form the following conclusion: in reality there are many individual wolves; the general concept of 'wolf' which I form in my mind does not, as such, exist. Only individual wolves actually exist in the world. Such a person is concluding, therefore, that the 'wolf concept' is not a reality. That is an example of someone who merely judges and forms opinions. What about the other person, who lets reality speak for itself? How will he think of that invisible quality of wolf which is to be found in every single wolf and which characterizes all wolves alike? His train of thought will perhaps be roughly as follows: 'I shall compare a wolf with a lamb; I am not going to formulate any judgement on the matter, though, but will simply let the facts speak to me.' And now let us imagine that this person has the opportunity to observe with his own eyes a wolf eating up a lamb. After this had happened he would have to recognize that the substance which had before been running about as a lamb was now inside the wolf, had been absorbed into the wolf.

It is a remarkable thing, though, that just perceiving this fact without judgement is enough to see the full reality of 'wolf nature'. External judgement might lead us to the conclusion that if a wolf were deprived of all other food and ate nothing but lamb, he must gradually, through a process of metabolism, replace his own substance with lamb substance. In fact, of course, he does not become a lamb, but keeps his own clothing and his own insides too! What this tells us, though, is that it is quite wrong to conclude that the material part of the wolf is all that constitutes 'wolf', that the concept 'wolf' has no reality. When we allow ourselves to be taught by the facts of the outer world, we can learn that the wolf is not just a configuration of matter before us, but also extends beyond what is visible; that in other words what we don't see is very real indeed. The aspect of the wolf which is not wholly submerged in the realm of matter is what prevents it becoming lamb when it eats nothing but lamb. All that has passed into the wolf from the lamb is of a material nature only.

It is sometimes difficult to draw a clear line between judging and letting reality speak to us. But once we have grasped the difference, once we only employ judgement for the practical purposes of everyday life, and approach a deeper truth and reality by allowing ourselves to be taught by what comes towards us, then we gradually arrive at a mood of soul which can show us the true meaning of 'surrender'. This is a state of mind which does not seek to investigate truth by projecting itself, but which opens itself to things so that they can reveal themselves, which can be patient, can wait until it is ripe for receiving this revelation. Applying judgement and forming opinions leads to a continual desire to arrive at truth at every step; surrender, in contrast, does not set out to force its way through into some truth or other. It is a state of mind which wishes to educate itself first, to wait patiently until a stage is reached at which the truth simply flows into us from the things of the world, revealing itself and filling our whole being.

And now we must go on to consider the fruits we receive from this surrender. What do we attain when our thinking has progressed from wonder to reverence, then from a sense of ourselves in wise harmony with reality to an attitude, finally, of humility and surrender?

As we go about the world and observe the green sprouting of plants, admire the wealth of colour in the blossoms, or as we contemplate the broad blue sky and the golden brilliance of the stars—not judging or forming opinions about these things, but allowing them to reveal themselves to us—if we have really reached this stage of surrender, all things in the world of sense become quite different for us than they were before: something is revealed to us within the sense-world which we can only describe with a word belonging to the realm of our feeling and soul-life. Let me show you what I mean in diagrammatic form:

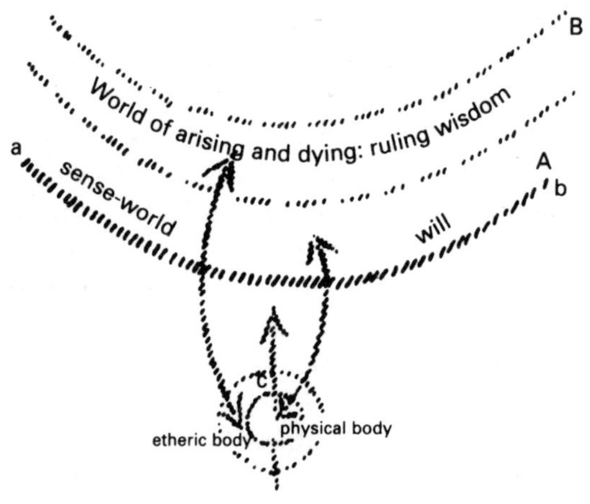

Suppose this line (a–b) represents the sense-world as it reveals itself to us. Imagine you are standing here (c) and you perceive the world of senses spread out before you like a veil. This line (a–b) is meant to represent the tones that enter your ears, the colours and forms that fall upon your eyes, the smells and tastes that affect your other organs, all the hardness, softness etc. of sense-impressions. In ordinary life we stand within the world of senses and apply to it our capacity for judgement. How else do all the sciences arise? People approach the world of senses and investigate with all sorts of methods the laws that are at work there. But you will by now have gathered that such a process can never lead us into the realm of reality, because judgement is not the right tool to lead us there. Only by educating our thinking, only by following a path which progresses through wonder, reverence etc., can we ever penetrate reality. Then the sense-world changes and becomes something quite new and different. It is vital that we discover this new quality if we are to recognize the real nature of the world of senses.

Let us imagine that a person who has developed the feeling and attitude of surrender to a high degree comes to the fresh, full green of a meadow. At first sight he cannot distinguish the colours of any individual plants but sees just a general overall freshness of green. Such a person will feel within himself, if he has really developed this feeling of surrender, an inner sense of balance—he cannot help it: he senses not a fixed but a living mood of balance, one we might compare with a gentle and even flow of water. He cannot help conjuring up this inner picture, this inner feeling of harmony. And it is the same with every taste and smell, with every sense-perception—each one calls up in his soul a feeling of inner movement and activity. There is no colour or tone that does not speak to him so that he responds with inner vitality and activity, not forming a judgement or opinion but answering what he perceives with inner activity and soul-resonance. The whole sense-world, to be brief, reveals itself to him in terms which he can only describe as *will*. Everything in the sense-world is will: strong, powerful currents of will. I really want to emphasize this point. Anyone who has attained a high degree of the quality of surrender finds that everything in the sense-world is composed of burgeoning will. Even a person who has developed only a slight degree of this attitude of surrender finds it troubling if he suddenly sees someone coming towards him wearing clothes in a brash or clashing colour. He cannot help experiencing inwardly, in inner movement and activity, all that comes towards him from without. He is always connected with the whole world through this will which he senses and feels in everything. And it is through this will-connection with the whole sense-world that he comes close to reality, begins to penetrate it. The sense-world thus becomes something like a sea of infinitely differentiated will, and this means that what we usually otherwise experience as something spread out around us acquires for us a certain density or depth. We begin to see and hear beyond and behind the surface of things, and what we see and hear is will, flowing, streaming will. I will also mention here, for those of you familiar with Schopenhauer, that he guessed at the presence of this burgeoning will, but only in a narrow, one-sided way, in the world of sound and tone. He described music as differentiated effects of will.[2] In fact the whole sense-world appears to the person who has learnt surrender to be composed of flourishing will.

But we can go further: once we have learned to sense the will streaming everywhere through the sense-world, we can as it were pass through the veil of the sense-world and penetrate the secrets behind and beyond it which are otherwise hidden from us.

To understand what follows we must first ask how it is that we gain any knowledge at all of the sense-world. The answer is simple: through our senses. Through the ear we acquire knowledge of the world of sounds, through the eye, knowledge of colour and form, etc. We know the sense-world because it is mediated to us through our sense organs. A person usually receives sense-impressions and then forms judgements on the basis of them. But the person who has learnt surrender senses the active, flourishing will streaming towards him through his sense-impressions. He feels as though he were swimming together with the things he perceives in a sea of active will. And once a person has attained this and feels the activity and sway of will in the things before him, then the force of his own evolution drives him on, as it were, to the next stage. This follows as a matter of course once the preceding stages have been passed through—of feeling oneself in harmony with the wisdom of the world, of reverence, of wonder.

All these stages, which culminate in that of surrender, give us the possibility of growing into, growing together with all things, through the body which stands beyond and behind the physical—our etheric body. We first grow together, grow into the things of the physical world with our physical body, our sense-organs enter into the active, streaming will. When we see, hear, smell etc., as people who have attained to surrender, we feel this will flowing into us through our eyes and ears, feel ourselves truly related to the things before us. But behind the physical eye and ear is the etheric eye and ear. Our etheric body permeates us thoroughly. And just as the physical body grows into the things of the sense-world through streaming, flourishing will, so too does the etheric body grow together with the sense-world. When this happens, though, a quite new way of seeing dawns in us. The world undergoes a still greater change for us than when we penetrate from outer sense-impression through to weaving, active will. When our etheric body grows together with the things of the world, they make an impression on us that makes it seem impossible for us to retain our old concepts and thoughts about them. They change in our perception as we enter into relation with them. Imagine a person who has already experienced the mood of surrender in his soul, who looks at a green leaf full of sap. He turns his soul-perception upon the thing in front of him, and at once finds that he cannot just leave this juicy green leaf as it is: the moment he beholds it he somehow has the feeling that it is growing out beyond itself. He senses that this green, sap-filled leaf has the potential to become something quite different. You know, of course, that we can observe a progression in the arrangement of leaves on a plant-stem, so that at last the highest leaves metamorphose into the coloured 'flower-leaf' or petal. The whole plant is really a transformed leaf, as Goethe described it.[3] So when such a person beholds a leaf he sees it is not complete, that it is trying to grow beyond itself; he sees in other words more than the green leaf actually shows him. The green leaf 'touches' him so that he senses within himself budding, sprouting life. He grows together with the burgeoning, sprouting life of the green leaf.

But now suppose he looks at the dry, hard bark of a tree. If he grows together with that, he cannot help falling under the sway of a mood of death. In the dry, withered bark he sees not more, but less than is there in reality, whereas someone who perceives it in an external way alone can admire it, find pleasure in it. At any rate he does not find in it that quality of shrivelling and withering that pierces the soul with a sense of death.

There is nothing in the whole world that does not, when the etheric body grows together with it, give rise to feelings either of growing, sprouting life, or of decaying and passing away. Imagine someone who has attained the stage of surrender and then progresses further, and turns his attention to the human larynx. He will have a strange impression: the larynx will appear to him as an organ in its evolutionary infancy, whose great future still lies before it. By observing the larynx so that it reveals its secrets to him, he will feel that it is like a seed, not at all like a fruit or something about to wither. From reading the secrets which the larynx itself reveals to him, he knows that a time will come in human evolution when the larynx will be wholly transformed, when its present function—to voice our words—will be transformed into a means for giving birth to the human being.[4] The larynx is the future organ of procreation and birth. At present we give birth to words through it, but in future this seed will develop the capacity to give birth to the whole human being once we have become spiritualized. The larynx itself reveals this when we allow it to speak its secret to us. Other organs of the body, in contrast, show us that they have long passed their zenith, and we can see that they will in future times no longer be present in the human organism.

Such faculties, then, have direct and immediate vision of both future waxing growth, and of future waning and dying away. Budding, sprouting life, and death and decay, are two aspects that we find intermingled with one another all around us when we attain a union of our etheric body with the world of reality. As we progress still further, this is something which begins to test us very severely. Each single being that we meet and that makes itself known to us will have certain aspects which arouse in us a feeling of burgeoning, sprouting life, and others which communicate a feeling of dying and waning. Everything which we perceive behind and beyond the sense-world reveals itself to us in one or other of these two fundamental aspects. In occultism this is called the world of arising and dying. Past the veil of the sense-world we see through into a world of arising and dying away; and behind this, wisdom works, weaves and reigns.

Behind active, reigning will, active wisdom holds sway. I say *active* wisdom, because the wisdom people usually imbue their concepts and ideas with is not active at all, but fixed in forms of thought. The wisdom we acquire when we look beyond and behind active, flourishing will is inwardly united with things, and in the realm of reality a wisdom holds sway whose workings come to real expression, a wisdom which is truly present and active. Wherever this wisdom draws back its forces from the world of reality, the dying process begins; where it flows into this world, you find things arising, budding, sprouting, waxing. We can mark off these worlds in the following way (see diagram): we look at the sense-world and see it first as *A*, and then we look at *B*, which is behind the sense-world—the world of active wisdom. From this world is derived the 'substance' of our etheric body. The active wisdom we can perceive outside ourselves can also be perceived within us, in our etheric body. And in our physical body we perceive not only what our senses show us, but also flourishing, active will—for this is to be found everywhere behind the outer world of the senses.

Yes, the remarkable thing is that when we attain to the stage of surrender and meet another person, the complexion of his skin and face—whether brighter or paler, whether more reddish or yellow—is something that we grow into; we grow together with the reality of, say, his rosy cheeks, and have access to the active will contained there. We see everything that lives and weaves in him shooting across to us through his rosy cheeks—a sign, for those who care to observe it, of blooming health. At this stage of surrender we perceive the active will in another person. And we may now say, turning to our diagram, that our physical body, denoted by this circle here, is taken from the world *A*, the world of active will. Our etheric body on the other hand, denoted by this second circle, is taken from the world of active wisdom, the world *B*. Here you have, then, the connection between the world of active wisdom that is spread before us, and our own etheric body; and between the world of active will that is spread before us, and our own physical body. In ordinary life we are not aware of these connections, we are deprived of the power to perceive them. The connections are there but the human being is separated from and can have no influence upon them.

Why is this? Actually there is a condition in which our thoughts and all the judgements we arrive at are not so harmless and unconnected with our reality as they usually are for our everyday existence. In our ordinary everyday waking state the good gods have seen to it that our thoughts cannot exert too damaging an influence on our own reality; they have withheld from us the power our thoughts might otherwise exercise over our physical and etheric bodies, and we and the world would really be in grave danger if this were not so. If human thoughts, let me emphasize this, were to have the significance that the thoughts of the gods have in reality, then every error we made would bring about a death process within us, and little by little we would become dried up husks. And as for lies! If every lie a person told burnt up the portion of his brain involved in it, which would be the case if he could intrude into the world of reality, his brain would not stand up to the treatment for long! The good gods have withheld from our soul the power over our etheric and physical bodies. But that cannot be so continually, without pause. For were our souls never able to have any influence on our physical and etheric bodies, we would very quickly consume the forces within them and would have only a very short life. For in our soul, as we shall see in the course of these lectures, are contained the forces that must flow ever and again into the physical and etheric bodies to sustain them. This inflow of forces takes place at night when we are asleep. From the universe, during the night when we sleep, flow rejuvenating streams through the ego and astral body into the etheric and physical bodies. This is the living connection between the worlds of will and wisdom, and our physical and etheric bodies. For it is into these worlds during sleep that our astral body and ego vanish. They enter into these worlds and there build up centres of attraction for the substances which need to stream from the world of wisdom into the etheric body, and from the world of will into the physical body. This happens during the night, for if we were conscious of this process and present in it, this instreaming would have devastating effects. If a person was conscious in sleep, with his normal everyday consciousness, with all his errors and vices, with all the bad deeds he may have done, this would form a strange trap or net for the forces which were supposed to flow into him. This would wreak dreadful destruction and havoc in his etheric and physical bodies as a result of the influences from the worlds of active wisdom and will being sent in a distorted form through his ego and astral body.

This is why the good gods have made sure that we cannot be conscious during the night when the right, health-giving forces stream into our physical and etheric bodies. They have dulled our consciousness during sleep so that we cannot cause damage and ruin, as we undoubtedly would if conscious. This is also why we have to undergo great hardship and pain on the path of knowledge, when we genuinely strive to ascend into higher worlds. In my book *Knowledge of the Higher Worlds* you can find a description of the way the sleeping state provides a means to help us rise from the world of outer reality into higher worlds. When we begin to illuminate our sleeping consciousness by drawing on the world of Imagination, when we can start to draw upon knowledge and experience which can light up the darkness of our sleeping state, then we must take great care to keep ourselves out of the way, to shut out from our consciousness all that might harm and disturb our physical and etheric bodies. It is absolutely necessary, in making the ascent to higher worlds, to know ourselves inside out. Once we really know ourselves, we mostly stop loving ourselves. Self-love usually comes to an end where self-knowledge begins; and this self-love (which is always present in someone who has not attained self-knowledge, for it is an illusion to imagine we do not love ourselves: we love ourselves more than anything else in the world) must be overcome if we are to be able to shut ourselves out of our consciousness. We must actually come to the point of being able to put ourselves, as we presently are, to one side. By attaining the level of surrender we have already done much, but we must now cease to love ourselves at all. I must always be capable of feeling the necessity for putting myself to one side, out of the picture, of shutting out completely all those aspects of myself which I otherwise feel quite at home with—errors, preconceptions, prejudices—whose forces would mingle with and muddy the pure stream which can enable me to develop clairvoyance. These disrupting, disturbing, destroying forces will otherwise pour into my physical and etheric bodies. As long as we are not conscious in sleep, as long as we cannot rise into the world of clairvoyance, the good gods protect us from such forces penetrating the streams which flow into our etheric and physical bodies from the worlds of will and wisdom. But when we raise our consciousness up into the realm of clairvoyance, the gods can no longer protect us—since their protection consists in dulling our consciousness. We must ourselves then lay aside all prejudice, sympathy, antipathy etc. We must put all these things firmly to one side, for if any self-love or personal desires remain in us, or if we are still liable to make judgements based on our own personal predilections, we can cause harm and damage to our physical and etheric bodies when ascending to higher worlds. It is enormously important to be clear about such things. We can then see how significant it is that in our normal waking lives we are protected from having any influence on our physical and etheric bodies through the fact that our thoughts, while we remain in the physical and etheric realm, exert no direct influence upon reality, and can therefore not provide us, either, with any immediate judgement about the nature of reality. If this were not so, every false thought would injure the physical and etheric bodies. In the night, though, if we were conscious, there would appear before us all that I have described: the sense-world as a sea of active will; and behind it, as though lashing it on and pouring through it, the wisdom which is the active, living fabric of the world, whose waves continually call forth the processes of arising and dying away. That is the true world into which we look, the world of active will and active wisdom, and this last is also the world of continual birth and death. It is in fact our world, which it is so important for us to perceive and recognize. For if we once recognize it, we begin truly to discover a means for attaining to ever greater heights of surrender, begin to feel ourselves interwoven with the realm of continual birth and death, and realize that every one of our actions connects us in some way with the world of arising and dying away. Then we perceive 'good' not just as something which pleases our personal tastes, towards which we feel personal sympathy, but as something that is active and creative in the universe, something that is always and everywhere arising and coming into being. And we perceive 'bad' as a continual influx of decay and disintegration, a constant dying away. We will then have made an important transition to a new view of the world in which we will only be able to picture evil as the destroying angel of death striding through the world, and good as the creator, as the source of continual birth, both great and small, throughout the universe. It is the science of the spirit which can awaken in us a sense of how we can deepen and spiritualize our whole outlook on life. It can help us feel strongly and deeply that the world of good and the world of bad are not merely as they appear to us in the external, illusory world we acknowledge with our earthly senses, making all our judgements about what most personally pleases or displeases us. We can instead begin to see that the world of good is the creative world, and that evil is the destroying angel with its scythe; and to see that every bad action of ours makes us an accomplice of this dark angel, that in fact we take up his scythe ourselves and become part of the processes of death and decay. The ideas we can gain from a spiritual foundation have a strengthening influence upon our whole outlook on life. This is the strength that humanity should now receive, so as to carry it forward into future evolution—for it will be sorely needed. Until now, the gods have taken care of human beings. Now, though, in this fifth post-Atlantean epoch, our destiny, our power for good and evil, will increasingly be handed over to us ourselves. It is therefore necessary to know what good and evil mean, and to recognize them in the world—the one as a creative, the other as a death-bringing principle.

II. ALL LIFE UNFOLDS BETWEEN THE POLARITIES OF LUCIFERIC AND AHRIMANIC FORCES

1. Christ, Ahriman and Lucifer in Relationship to the Human Being[1]

Good morning to you! Have you thought of anything you would like us to discuss today?

Questioner: Could you, Dr Steiner, please say something about the relationship of Christ, Ahriman and Lucifer to the human being?

First we'll have to look at things from a slightly different angle, otherwise you will feel that what I have to say is unfounded superstition. Let's remind ourselves firstly of things we have already discussed.

Nowadays, you see, people think that the nature of the human being is single and uniform. But it is not. We are caught up in a continual process of life flourishing, then dying away. We do not just start to live at birth and die at death but, as I have often said, we are continually dying then reviving again.

If we look at the human head, for instance, we can see that its inner composition is entirely nerve-substance. Nerve 'threads' run throughout the rest of the body but the inside of the head itself is all nerve. In a drawing it will look something like this (see over). Inside, the head and the forehead are all nerve, a thick mass of nerves; some of this nerve-mass runs down through the spinal column, and from there it radiates out through the whole body. These threads running everywhere through the body are concentrated in the head in a uniform mass of nerves.

The inside of the human stomach, for example, has very many nerves. The solar plexus situated there contains a great deal of nerve substance. But this is true also of the arms, hands, legs and feet, into which many nerve-threads pass.

If we then turn our attention from the nerves to the blood

vessels, we find that those in the head are rather delicate and fine, while in the heart-region they are particularly well developed; and in the limbs they become strong and thick. So we can see that there are two distinct and separate systems, developed differently in different parts of the body: the nervous system and the blood-vessel system.

The fact is, you see, that we are continually being reborn through our blood, every day, every hour. Blood renews us constantly. If we only had a blood-system we would always grow, grow larger, grow more vital. If on the other hand we only had a nervous system, we would continually be exhausting ourselves and dying away. These two opposite tendencies are continually at work in us simultaneously: the nervous system which ages us constantly, which leads us continually towards death; and the blood-vessel system, connected with processes of nourishment, which constantly rejuvenates us.

We can pursue this theme further: in old age, as you know, many people become sclerotic or, we may say, 'calcified' or hardened. People who suffer from a hardening of the arteries find it more difficult to move properly. When this arterial sclerosis becomes very pronounced, people may often be debilitated by a stroke.

But what does this process of hardening, of sclerosis, tell us? It is really as though a person's blood vessels were trying to become nerve. The nerves have to die away continually all through our lives; they have to partake of a process which would be quite wrong for our blood vessels. Blood vessels should remain vital and vigorous, while nerve-functions require a continual dying-away process. A person whose nerves are too soft, not 'hardened' enough, can become insane. In other words the nerves and blood-vessels must be quite different from each other to function properly.

So we cannot avoid recognizing the fact that there are two principles simultaneously at work in us, which oppose each other. Our nervous system makes us grow continually older through the day. During the night fresh life is restored through the blood. It is like the swinging of a pendulum: growing old, growing young again, growing old, growing young again. Except that each day that passes allows a little more 'age' to accrue in spite of the good work of the night, until enough age has accrued and we finally die altogether.

These two opposing principles in the human being, and the balance between them, have far-reaching consequences for him. If the forces of youth and vitality are too overweening, people can develop pleurisy or pneumonia. Things which are good and right in their proper sphere become tendencies to illness if they get out of proportion. Illness always appears when aspects which have their right and proper place get out of hand and impinge too far on the state of balance. Fever appears when the rejuvenating processes become too strong: our whole body starts to be *too* vigorous and vital.

Imbalance between these polarities also effects our emotional and mental life. Just as the body can either become too feverish or too sclerotic, so too can our souls. People have a certain tendency they don't much like to hear spoken of, since it is so widespread nowadays, to become fixed and pedantic. A school-teacher, for instance, may easily become dried-up and pedantic, though he really needs to be flexible and enthusiastic. This is a similar phenomenon in soul-life to the physical hardening of the arteries. But we can also become too soft in our souls, in which case we become cloud-cuckoo-land dreamers. We may then turn to mysticism or theosophy, so as to avoid the need to think properly, so as to allow our imagination to transport us into other worlds without having to hone our thinking. That is the same tendency that bodily fever expresses. Becoming a mystic or a theosophist is the same as getting a high temperature.

We need both tendencies. We cannot understand or enter into anything without the power of imagination; and we cannot bring any order into our lives without a little bit of pedantry, without keeping some kind of record and account of things. What it comes down to is the balance, the right proportion.

Our spirit itself is also caught up in these two tendencies. Just consider what happens when we wake up from sleep, actually a very sudden change. We lie there, quite unaware of our surroundings—someone may even tickle us without waking us. Then we suddenly wake up, and see and hear everything. This is really an enormous change in our condition, and we need the power, the force which allows us to wake. But it can become too strong if, for instance, we cannot fall asleep, if we are plagued by insomnia.

There are also people who never really wake up properly. They spend their lives in a sort of twilight state of dream, and would always prefer to be asleep. Of course we need the capacity to fall asleep—but not to such a degree that we can never wake up properly.

Let's sum up then: we can distinguish certain polar tendencies in the human being on three different levels. On the one hand is the nervous system, which continually tends towards hardening and calcification. All of you—with the exception of one little fellow sitting there—are old enough for your nervous system to have grown a little calcified. If your nerves were still as soft as they were when you were six months old, you would all be insane. Mad people have an over-soft, young child's nervous system. We need this tendency towards hardening and calcification. On the other hand we also need in its proper sphere the tendency to rejuvenation and softening.

Body	hardening calcification	softening rejuvenation

In our emotional life, in the realm of soul, we can say that hardening corresponds to pedantry, philistinism, materialism, dry reason. Which we need in the right dosage! If we didn't have something of these qualities we'd be flibbertigibbets—all over the place. If we had no trace of pedantry we wouldn't put our clothes away in the right drawer; we'd be more likely to put them in the oven or hang them up in the chimney! We need imagination, but not to the extent of lifting off into cloud-cuckoo land; and we need a little pedantry, but not so that we become fixed and fossilized.

I once knew someone who hated imagination and the imaginary to the extent that he never went to the theatre, let alone the opera, for he said that it was all untrue. He had no spark of imagination. So you can see that without it, one can turn into a very dry sort of specimen, someone who scuttles through life, rather than a real, full-blooded person.

Soul:	pedantry philistinism materialism dry reason	fantasy dreaming mysticism theosophy

In terms of our spirit, we can recognize the tendency towards hardening in the process of awakening. When we wake up, we grasp firm hold of the body, start to use our limbs. The opposite tendency, towards softening, expresses itself when we fall asleep, when we sink into dreams. Then we let go of the body.

Spirit	waking up	falling asleep

You can see, then, that we are constantly in danger of swinging too far in one or other of these directions. A magnet, as you know, attracts iron; but there are two aspects of this process, a positive and negative magnetism. One attracts, the other repulses. In the realm of physical phenomena we aren't in the least embarrassed to call a spade a spade, to name what we observe. I have now described the same polar tendencies in three different realms: physical, soul and spirit. You can understand and recognize what I'm saying and observe it yourselves. But to do so, it is necessary to call things by their names. When observing positive magnetism, we must be clear that it is not the iron itself that brings about this effect, but something working invisibly within the iron.

Whoever refuses to contemplate such an idea can't see much further than the end of his own nose. He is likely to say that magnetic attraction in the iron is codswallop. 'What's all this nonsense about magnetism?' he may exclaim. 'That's just iron, nothing more nor less—I shoe my horse with it, there's nothing more to say.' This is, of course, a rather pedestrian and idiotic view of things, for the iron horse-shoe can have further aspects beyond its apparent function.

In the same way, the process of hardening and calcification contains an invisible, supersensible, essential aspect that it is possible to observe if one develops the capacity to do so. This aspect is called 'ahrimanic'. The ahrimanic forces are the ones which continually strive to make us into a sort of dried-up corpse. If only ahrimanic powers were at work, we would calcify, shrivel up and fossilize. We would be continually wide awake and unable to fall asleep.

The opposite forces of rejuvenation and softening, of imagination and fantasy, are the 'luciferic' forces. We need them so that we don't become corpses. But if only luciferic forces existed we would stay children all our lives. We need both tendencies—without the luciferic we would be old and ancient at the age of three; without the ahrimanic we would be eternal children.

	ahrimanic	*luciferic*
body:	hardening calcification	softening rejuvenation
soul:	pedantry philistinism materialism dry reason	fantasy dreaming mysticism theosophy
spirit:	waking up	falling asleep

These two kinds of opposing tendency must be balanced out and harmonized. How can this come about? Neither tendency should get the upper hand.

We are now in the year 1923; and since the turning point of time, when our AD time reckoning began, up to this present moment, humanity has been exposed to the danger of unbalanced ahrimanic forces. Education, these days, except where the science of the spirit is at work, has a decidedly ahrimanic tendency. When our children come to school they have to learn things that actually seem very alien, even comical to them, things they can have no real interest in at all. They know, for instance, what their fathers are like and what their hair, eyes, nose etc. look like. And then they come to school and have to learn that these alien signs: F-A-T-H-E-R are supposed to represent the father they know. The same is true of everything which children are supposed to learn at school. It is all quite alien to them.

This is a good reason for establishing schools in which

children can learn things they relate to, which they have an interest in. If education were to continue in its present tracks, people would soon start to grow prematurely old, to lose all flexibility, because this form of education is ahrimanic. In these last nineteen hundred years our whole evolutionary tendency has been in this ahrimanic direction. Previously it was different.

If you look back, from 8,000 years BC until the turning point of time, people were exposed to the opposite danger, of being unable to grow old. In those ancient days, schools as we know them now did not exist. The only schools were for those who had attained a respectable age and who were to become scholars. There were no schools for children in those times, for they just learned what they needed to from life itself. No one tried to teach children things which were alien to their nature. So there was an opposite danger: of people becoming too luciferic, too cloud-cuckoo-ish and dreamy. These were times, it is true, of great wisdom, but there was a need for this luciferic tendency to be harnessed, reined in; otherwise people would just have wanted to tell each other airy nothings or ghost stories all day long.

In other words: from 8,000 BC until the turning point of time was a luciferic age. From then on, until our present time, has been an ahrimanic epoch.

Let's just look for a moment at the earlier, luciferic age. The scholars of those days were rather concerned about the particular human tendencies apparent then. These scholars lived in tower-like structures. The Tower of Babel mentioned in the Bible was just one of these 'ivory towers'. The scholars lived and learned there. They were aware of their luciferic powers of imagination and fantasy, yet also of the fact that their observation of external phenomena could balance these powers. They observed the motion of the stars, for instance, and recognized that these accorded with certain laws that were not subject to their desires or imagination. They were aware that if, for instance, they imagined a tiny piece of wood being lit and blazing up in an enormous incandescence, this would not be born out by the actual results, that in fact a small piece of wood would only produce a small fire. The aim of these ancient schools was actually to harness and rein in people's over-burgeoning powers of fantasy and imagination. Their worry and concern was that everyone else was denied this subjection of their fantasy to objective law, since only relatively few could become scholars. So they dispensed their wisdom and teachings—yet much of what they taught was just to damp down the people's capacity for luciferic fantasy, and did not always relate to truth. There was a good deal of dross mixed with the gold, and in fact it is the dross which mainly survived from these old teachings.

And if we then turn to the age in which we are now, the ahrimanic age, we can see that our modern science has increasingly turned towards the ahrimanic and atomistic. This science has become something which makes us rather dry and arid, for it takes only the physical, material, calcified world into account.

Between these two poles stands a third, mediating quality, which we can call the truly Christian. My dear friends, true Christianity is something too little known in the world. The worldly Christianity we are familiar with is something quite different, that we must actually oppose.

The Being I spoke to you of last time,[2] who was born at the turning point of time and lived for thirty three years, was not as people describe Him. He wanted to dispense to all humanity teachings which would allow people to balance opposing ahrimanic and luciferic tendencies. The true meaning of Christianity lies in striving for this balance. What people nowadays often think of as being Christian is really not what is intended.

What, for example, does Christianity imply in the physical realm, in the sphere of illness and health? It implies gaining a real knowledge of the human being, so that if a person succumbs to pleurisy we can see that he is too subject to luciferic influences. Once I know this, I can start to try to balance the scales:

In the case of pleurisy, the ahrimanic is too weak, so I must add an 'ahrimanic ingredient' to the situation, to provide balance. One thing I can do is the following: I take a piece of pear-wood, a plant which has strong, vigorous growth in spring. The wood nearest the bark is best, for it contains the strongest growth forces. I now kill off these forces by burning the wood to charcoal, thus 'ahrimanizing' the rejuvenated powers of the pear-tree. Then I grind this charcoal into powder and administer it to the person suffering from pleurisy through an excess of luciferic forces. So I have added an ahrimanic ingredient to an over-luciferic condition, and created more of a balance. I have mineralized, and so also ahrimanized the pear wood by charcoaling it.

Or let us assume that a person acquires a tired, wan countenance, so that it seems likely he may soon suffer a stroke. The scales in this case are tipped too far towards the ahrimanic, and we must redress the balance by administering to him something of a luciferic quality. How would I do this?

Let us observe a plant: the root is hard and contains minerals and salts—not at all luciferic. The stem and leaves are not luciferic either, but if I proceed upwards, I find a sweet-smelling blossom. This is sending out substance from itself, into the cosmos—otherwise I would not be able to smell

it. So from this blossom I extract its juice, which has a luciferic quality. This I administer in the right way, so that the balance is redressed: I heal the patient by counteracting a preponderance of the ahrimanic tendency.

How, in contrast, does modern medicine proceed? It experiments. A chemist discovers, say, acetylphenidine—we don't need to know exactly what that is, it's a complicated substance. Then it is taken to the hospital, where it is perhaps tried out on 30 or so patients. Then their reactions, temperature etc. are noted, and if there is some result the substance is used as a medicine.

But people have little idea what's really going on inside the human body. There's no understanding of the inner processes at work. The only right way forward is for people to realize that pleurisy, for example, indicates too pronounced a luciferic tendency which must be balanced by the ahrimanic; or that a stroke points to a preponderance of the ahrimanic, which must be redressed by the luciferic. This sort of approach is what humanity needs, for it is at present not Christian enough in this respect. Christianity is the balance, is seeking to establish a balance and harmony. This applies also to medicine and healing, on a very physical, practical level.

This is what I also wished to express in this wooden figure of Christ,[3] intended for the Goetheanum building. Above you see Lucifer, the luciferic, representing everything that has to do with fever, imagination, falling asleep etc.; below you find all the tendencies to hardening, the ahrimanic. And between these two stands Christ.

Looking upon this figure will help us know how to proceed in all sorts of different realms: from medicine to science to sociology. Nowadays we should start to become aware of how luciferic and ahrimanic tendencies are at work in human nature.

But do people have, or want to have, any inkling of these things? Not so long ago there was a priest, renowned in Basel and still further afield, called Frohnmeyer, who held lectures all over the place. He did not actually take the trouble to come and see this sculpture himself, but read someone else's account (who had also, perhaps, not bothered to take a look at it). This did not stop him pronouncing on this figure of Christ, and saying that Steiner, over in Dornach, was making a dreadful travesty: a Christ figure whose upper parts had luciferic features; and below, animal traits.

You can see for yourselves that this is wrong: the Christ figure has a very human head. But the priest confused the matter. He did not even know that the sculpture is still unfinished below—not so much animal forms as an unhewn lump of wood! But he was, after all, a priest, someone who strives for truth, and so the whole world now believes that what he reported must be true. It is very hard to make any headway in such circumstances, when people have no wish to see or hear the truth. People would rather take their truth from the mouths of priests, yet in this case this has led to a lie of appalling proportions. But this is not quite the end of the story—it's extraordinary the way some people think. At the time that Frohnmeyer wrote these things, we had Dr Boos with us here at the Goetheanum. You probably know that Dr Boos likes to take up the cudgels on occasion; you may think that cudgels are a bit hard—rather ahrimanic—and that perhaps one should just resort to a softer method—a few soft, luciferic strokes with a feather-duster perhaps. Anyway, for better or worse, Dr Boos let him have it with the cudgels, told him the truth in no uncertain terms. And who receives a letter from Frohnmeyer? I do! I get a long letter from Frohnmeyer complaining about Dr Boos' behaviour and asking *me* to restrain his excesses.

Extraordinary the way people think! They attack someone, indulge in calumny against him, then afterwards ask that same person's protection against someone who tries to rectify the deceit.

It is a sign of the superficiality and meanness of our times, I'm afraid, that the general public don't rely on their own judgement enough in many matters, but just accept what those in positions of authority place before them.

What is needed is to open up a whole new stream and direction of thought. People need to realize that talking about Christianity until the cows come home is not going to get us very far. Instead we must make it real in a practical, down-to-earth way. We must know that medicine, for instance, can become Christian. If someone has eaten sugar continuously throughout his life, from childhood on, and as a result develops liver cancer, which is an ahrimanisation of the liver, we must know how to treat it by administering something containing luciferic qualities. Just as a person can distinguish between warm and cold, we must learn to distinguish between luciferic and ahrimanic tendencies. When our limbs grow stiff, we are becoming ahrimanic. We can counteract this by applying warm wraps and cloths, with something warming and of a luciferic nature. This is just an example of a whole approach, a whole way of understanding the human being so that medicine becomes Christian.

Pedagogy and education must become Christian in the same way. We must educate children without making them prematurely old from infancy. To do this we need to let them begin with things which are close to them, which they relate naturally to, which they are interested in, etc.

It is clear then, I hope, that the expressions I have used—ahrimanic, luciferic, Christian—are not unfounded superstition. They are actually truly scientific.

Let us look now, for a moment, at an aspect of our historical and cultural development. From the earliest days of Christianity, through to the twelfth, thirteenth and fourteenth centuries, Christians were actually forbidden to read the Bible, the New Testament. Only the priests were allowed to read it, not the congregations of believers. Why? Because the priests and scholars knew that it was necessary to read the Bible in the proper way. It was composed in a time in which people did not think in the way they do today, but much more in pictures and images. If people read it in the wrong way, without the proper preparation, they would soon discover that the four Gospels contradict one another. Why do they? Of course they do! Even in the fourth and fifth centuries, anyone who had all his wits would have been able to understand why this was.

Just imagine that I take a photograph of Herr Burle from the front and show you the picture. You will of course recognize him. But if someone comes along and takes a profile shot, and shows that to you, you might all refuse to believe it was Herr Burle, for the angle of the picture would show you an aspect you were not familiar with. Yet it would of course still be him. And if I photographed him from behind, you might all say: 'That can't be Herr Burle, he has a nose, not just hair!'

In the same way, one can 'photograph' a spiritual process from various different angles, which each appear quite different from one other. The four Evangelists are simply describing things from four different angles. But as times changed people stopped thinking there was any need to prepare themselves for reading the Gospels, or for doing anything else. They believed that school-training was a preparation enough for everything else, that by the age of 14 or 15 they should have no more need to prepare but ought to be able to understand everything. This sort of belief is what leads people to look upon our Goetheanum here, and say: 'Old, bald-headed people are going in there to learn. It's a school for the elderly—it must be a madhouse!' They say such things because they cannot imagine that older people might still want and need to learn. But we must be clear that we cannot read the Gospels properly without proper preparation, without beginning to understand that they embody a kind of picture language. If one wanted to read a piece of Chinese, one would have to learn the Chinese characters; in the same way, the Gospels will be gobbledygook to us if we don't learn to read them in the right way. Similarly, to understand things aright, we must learn to recognize that Christianity has everything to do with creating the right balance between luciferic and ahrimanic, so that neither tendency gains the upper hand at the expense of the other.

It is for this reason that anthroposophy is not ashamed to speak of Christianity in these terms. It emphasizes that Christianity is not served by uttering the word Christ all the time. People often accuse anthroposophy of mentioning Christ too little. But I reply that anthroposophy refrains from speaking of Christ because it remembers the Ten Commandments, specifically the one which says: 'Thou shalt not take the name of the Lord thy God in vain.' A Christian priest, nowadays, is likely to speak the name of Christ a great number of times throughout his sermon. But one should only speak this name when one really has some understanding for what it means! This is what distinguishes anthroposophy from a superstition or pretend piety. Anthroposophy aims to be nothing if not scientific. And it is in these terms that it views the Event in Palestine, which took place at the turning point of time, at the knife-edge between the ancient times which were luciferic, and the new times which are ahrimanic, as an occurrence of universal historical significance.

Only when we start to understand what really took place at that time on the earth will we be able to come into our true inheritance, come to ourselves. Nowadays people are quite 'outside' themselves, in the external views of science. We will speak further of these things next Wednesday at nine o'clock.[4] This, for now, is my answer to the question. I hope that it has shed some light on the whole subject.

2. The Relation of Ahrimanic and Luciferic Beings to the Normally Evolved Hierarchies

Today and during the next few days I should like to draw from our recent studies some conclusions about human life itself.[1] I will first deal with certain ideas which the outside world has about anthroposophy, showing what attitudes we should develop towards them, how we should respond.

All people nowadays recognize and acknowledge, though only in the sphere of nature and the natural world, the very same understanding which we wish through an anthroposophical science of the spirit to promote in the sphere of the life of spirit, the spiritual sphere. It would be a mistaken interpretation of the anthroposophical outlook to want to infuse it with outdated, erroneous forms of mysticism and superstition. We must accustom ourselves to using the terms and concepts that have become familiar to us for the realm of spirit, such as ahrimanic and luciferic, with the same precision and focus that a scientist will use when speaking of positive and negative electricity, magnetism and so on, though of course it is a different, higher realm that we are examining. But in contrast to the prevailing preconceptions of science, we should be aware that in opening up the world of spirit to our observation, all abstract, fixed concepts of the kind which ordinary science clings to must give way to a more real, living and spiritual kind of understanding.

Between birth and death, as we know, human beings have what we call a physical body; in addition they also have the so-called etheric body, or to use a slightly more accessible expression, a body of formative forces; then comes the astral body, which has a certain degree of consciousness, but not to the extent of our modern waking consciousness. What many people nowadays call the subconscious approximates to our astral body. Then comes what we think of as our normal level of consciousness which alternates between waking and sleeping states. It only enters into our awareness during sleep in the shape of chaotic dreams; in waking life it is not content with merely perceiving things but has recourse also to abstract judgements and concepts. This is the aspect of the human being which we call the ego or 'I', which is the only one, nowadays, of which we are really aware. This ego is reflected back to us in our consciousness, and within it is enacted all the thinking, feeling and willing of our souls. Everything else—astral body, etheric body and the physical body in its true form—lies below our consciousness and also below our ego. All that ordinary science—anatomy, physiology etc.—has to say about the physical body applies to its outer aspect alone, which is nothing more really than our conscious awareness of the physical body, which we obtain in the same way as any other sense-perception. This is the outer image of the physical body in our consciousness, not the physical body itself.

So the three constituent parts or members of the human being which we ascribe to pre-earthly evolution—you know something of this evolutionary process from my book *Occult Science*—are beyond the sphere of human consciousness. You will remember that proceeding from the human being into higher realms we find a hierarchy of beings above him, just as proceeding downwards we find the three realms of the animal, plant and mineral kingdom. When we examine the human being from a spiritual perspective, we can no longer confine ourselves to considering only those aspects of the astral, etheric and physical body which ordinary science takes into account—and with which anthroposophy, too, is concerned when it looks at that aspect of human life which unfolds in the sense-perceptible world. Earlier this autumn I spoke of the fact that these, let us call them lower aspects of human nature, are in fact intimately connected with the spirits of the various hierarchies.[2]

Recalling what I recently described to you in connection

with Goethe's world-view,[3] we can say that we are connected to certain spiritual forces underlying our evolution through the fact that we evolve through time by means of our three constituent aspects or bodies, are involved in a process of evolution from birth to death. I tried to clarify this with the following diagrammatic explanation:

If we think of this (see drawing) as our present condition, we must imagine it connected from its evolutionary past with the spiritual powers we have acknowledged as belonging to the higher hierarchies. As you know, in a normal person these spiritual powers, with the exception of the spirits of form, the exusiai, do not work directly within the ego. Apart from these spirits of form who endow us with our particularly human shape, the other spiritual forces do not work through or enter into our modern consciousness.

We can get a vague though workable idea of these spirits of form if we look at just one aspect of our overall shaping and structure—one which our physical body actually acquires during life. We all crawl to begin with, do not at first have the power to stand upright. The upright posture, or rather the force which makes this the right and true one for us, is vitally important in our whole being. Even the purely external difference between man and the animals does not, as people usually believe, consist so much in the number of bones and muscles, which are anyway roughly similar, as in this vertical force which gives the growing human being his form. This is only part of the difference, it is true, yet it is an essential part. This power of verticality that influences our physical development, is part and parcel of the forces which endow us earthly human beings with the form we have.

At a different level other forces are at work: those of cosmic movement, cosmic wisdom and cosmic will, which we call dynamis, kyriotetes and thrones, using ancient terms in a modern sense and spirit. These forces intervene in the unconscious parts of our being—those therefore that belong to the astral body, the etheric or body of formative forces, and the physical body. So when these component aspects of our being are observed without the spiritual content and connections to which I have referred, they appear as mere illusions or phantoms. We do not really inhabit external appearance, but the spiritual forces I have described.

Now as I recently mentioned in regard to Goethe's world-view, there are forces which work upon us for a time without being directly involved in our evolution. We call these two forces luciferic and ahrimanic: the luciferic works, we can say, more spiritually (see red in diagram), the ahrimanic more through the subconscious (mauve in diagram):

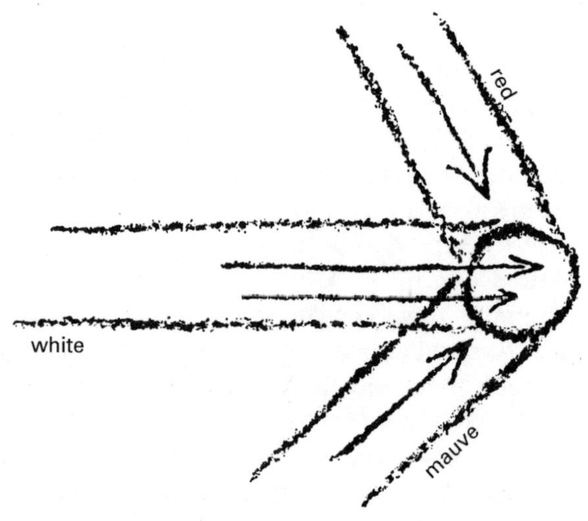

So the human being's participation in existence takes place through a threefold cosmic stream: there are forces connected directly with his onward path of evolution. Then there are also two other kinds of forces, luciferic and ahrimanic, which do not have a direct connection with his evolutionary path, but which exert an influence on his temporal existence, forming an inherent part of what constitutes him.

Now when we observe life we do not actually see the current of forces which belongs to us, but instead what has formed as a result of the confluence of these three streams. Whatever aspect of life we view—whether the outer sense-world or our more inward life, that charts a course between pleasure and pain, sorrow and joy, action and inaction—we always see these three streams indistinguishably interwoven. In contrast to a chemist for example, who tries to find out more about water than its straightforward appearance tells him by separating it into hydrogen and oxygen, we do not usually separate things out in ordinary life. But the science of the spirit must undertake this sort of spiritual chemistry, must analyse things into their constituent parts, for otherwise we will never manage to fathom human life.

We have examined the specific character and nature of what we call luciferic, and what we call ahrimanic, from all sorts of different angles. But now we need to look at these things once more from yet another point of view, and examine their direct influence upon human life. We must ask at what point in life luciferic influences are particularly strong and active, and likewise at what stage ahrimanic forces exert their strongest influence.

We cannot rely solely upon the stream of evolution and development which flows from our own innate being. You will remember from our previous discussions that we would not begin to attain any self-knowledge until we had reached middle age[4] if we were not exposed to the periodic influence of luciferic and ahrimanic powers. We *are* exposed to this influence, in fact we depend on it. In the whole realm we can characterize as conscious—not the natural endowment of consciousness, but everything which is more than just 'given' (such as developing some degree of self-knowledge in the first half of our lives, or striving to attain a greater awareness than we otherwise have)—there is an element we would have to call sur-conscious.* If this was not so, our consciousness would be of a quite different quality and nature. Sur-consciousness is what enables humanity to form its history in a more intentional way than would be possible if people were dependent on their purely physical evolution alone. Our culture today would look altogether different if this particular quality of human consciousness had been absent. Yet it is this sur-conscious which allows luciferic powers to exert their influence. If they did not, people would never even have dreamed of developing a form of thinking different from the one I recently described to you as the Goethean ideal. The luciferic forces allow people to form hypotheses, build up imaginative pictures and fantasies which may have little connection with reality. We do not only grasp reality, but also construct all kinds of ideas about reality which ultimately enable us to form a stronger, deeper connection with it than we otherwise would. Just think of the whole realm of art, in which the sur-conscious is of great importance, in which a luciferic influence is vital, unless we are happy to see art descend to mere naturalism. It is simply not possible, as I have emphasized many times, to reject all luciferic influences. If we did this our lives would grow shallow and unreal—we'd all become arch-philistines. It is the vitality and energy of the luciferic tendency in the human being that time and again provides us with the yeast to rise above pedantry and philistinism.

But this luciferic energy at the same time causes people to view the world from an aerial perspective, like birds high above the earth. All the wonderful programmes for turning the world into a better place, all those beautiful ideas for bringing about some kind of golden age, arise through the

* In contrast to subconscious. Sur = above or higher, as in surmount, surreal (transl.).

luciferic streams flowing into us. Every tendency to extricate ourselves from a rooted connection with reality, to spread our wings and soar above our actual circumstances, points to the influence of the luciferic. Another luciferic aspect of human nature is to lose interest in our fellow-men. Our interest in others would be far, far greater if we adhered only to our original, innate nature, to the evolutionary forces that truly belong to us. It is the luciferic element in us that diverts our interest away from other people. We should be aware—and a study of the true nature of the human being would show us this—that the world would be a very different place if we recognized the real origin of our absorbing interest in our own backyard, and of our far too meagre interest in the thoughts, feelings and will of others. We can only acquire a proper knowledge of the human being by lifting up this question into our consciousness: What is it that impels me to lose interest in other people? To understand why this is so will be a necessary future task of self-knowledge and culture. People today think that knowledge of the human being is just an arbitrary, personal kind of thing, that anyone's opinion, imagination or belief about what people are, or should be like, is perfectly valid. Seeing human nature for what it truly is and being clear that everyone, just in their 'unimproved', ordinary state—yes, even the criminal—actually has more to tell us about the real nature of the world than our most elevated fancies and beliefs about the human being, establishes the right equilibrium in us, counteracts the sway of the luciferic.

To strive for this kind of knowledge about the human being would reveal an enormous amount. Yet we have never been less interested in a real, genuine perception of human nature than we are today at our present stage of earthly evolution. This does not mean that we should have a wholly uncritical attitude towards human beings. Anyone who clings to the premise that all people are good and should all be loved equally is making things luciferically comfortable for himself, for his fantasy alone is operating. To regard all people as equal is pure luciferic fantasy; the point is not to cherish a general idea but to penetrate to the actual reality of every individual, and to develop a loving (or, perhaps more accurately, an interested) understanding for each specific instance of humanity.

You may wonder what good this luciferic tendency in us is if it hinders us from being tolerant and understanding of human nature, and from being interested in others. Yet it does have its proper place in the spirit's ordered household, if I can use such a pedestrian expression. We need this luciferic force for if we just flowed on, as it were, in the ongoing stream of our innate evolution, and were therefore never sidetracked away from a natural and spiritual perception and knowledge of every human being, we would—excuse the expression—drown in our knowledge. We would sink in it instead of coming properly to ourselves. There is nothing, actually, in our existence—and this is connected with many secrets of this existence—which does not turn to evil and misfortune if pursued to its ultimate consequence. The impulse which draws us to other people, which allows us to empathize with and relate to others in a warm and human way, is the same one that would allow us to drown in our perceptions and knowledge of others if the luciferic pinprick was not constantly there to remind us, to pull us up from drowning, to draw us back up to the surface so that we come back to ourselves and reawaken our self-interest. Particularly in the realm of relationships with other people we live in a continual alternation between our own innate forces and the luciferic ones. And if anyone believes it would be better for us just to follow our own evolutionary stream without being influenced by the luciferic, it is like saying that we should weigh things on a pair of scales by taking away one of the two pans, and using just one. Life takes its course through alternating, balancing conditions, not in absolute or fixed states. So we can see that the luciferic tendency impinges on our consciousness by mingling the sur-conscious with it.

The ahrimanic tendency, on the other hand, exerts its influence chiefly in the subconscious. Ahrimanic forces infiltrate all the subconscious, often subtle impulses in our nature. We could characterize and distinguish Ahriman and Lucifer by saying that the latter is a proud Spirit who likes to soar away into the heights of lofty vision, whereas the former is a more 'down-in-the-dumps', lonely Spirit, who does not readily make his presence known. Ahriman works upon our subconscious, is active there, conjures up judgements and opinions from it. People often believe that their opinions and decisions are formed consciously, but in fact they frequently make judgements on the basis of subconscious drives, instincts and subtle impulses; or simply allow them to be conjured up by these ahrimanic forces themselves.

Religions as we know have often derived their beliefs and descriptions from ancient, now faded, clairvoyant capacities. The disciple Peter was right to call Ahriman a 'prowling lion seeking whom he might devour'; he really does prowl in the hidden, subconscious realm of our being. He strives to attain his ends by diverting our subconscious forces to himself, to use them for different world-evolutionary purposes than would lie in our natural disposition and development.

If we look at the course of human history, we can see that luciferic forces are at work wherever far-reaching visions and programmes are hatched out which fail to reckon with the reality of human nature. What a vast number of ideas and ideals have been imagined for achieving humanity's happiness! And those who devise them are always firmly convinced that their plans alone will lead to this happiness. This is because such luciferic thinking soars aloft like the albatross, and takes no account of all that remains below, of all the actual convolutions and intricacies of life, believing that a bird's eye view of things can sort it all out. Such ideas of how to make the world a better place always rely on a defective knowledge of the human being and are invariably luciferic in nature. Dreams of world-power, on the other hand, which arise in fragmented, separate realms of human activity, are of an ahrimanic kind. Such dreams form in the subconscious. It is ahrimanic to wish to bring the whole world under the sway of one particular, circumscribed sphere of human life or activity. All that expresses a lust for power, for ruling over others, all that opposes healthy, human, social impulses, is of an ahrimanic nature. A person who loses interest in his fellow human beings can be said, not in a vaguely mystical way but in a precise sense, to be possessed by Lucifer; a person possessed by Ahriman, on the other hand, wishes to have as many people as possible under his thumb, and to rule over them—if he is clever enough—by using and manipulating their weaknesses. It is ahrimanic to delve in the sub-earthly, in the subconscious, to seek out human weakness in order to use it to rule over people.

But we must ask about the origin of all this. What is the real nature of ahrimanic and luciferic forces? We know that our earth is, to use a Goethean expression, a metamorphosis of previous planetary bodies, the fourth metamorphosis in fact. And to describe them we have said that the earth was first embodied in a Saturn incarnation, then proceeded through a Sun, then Moon embodiment, and finally reappeared as our Earth-stage. So the earth is the fourth incarnation of its cosmic being, the fourth metamorphosis, and will continue to pass through further stages of transformation. We need to remember this if we ask what significance the forces of the luciferic and ahrimanic beings have for us and the whole of cosmic evolution. We know that the spirits of form are connected with the form which the part of the cosmos we are most immediately involved with—our earth—has assumed. And if we examine a particularly characteristic aspect of the forces at work in our earth's formation we can discover that they are the same as are present in microcosmic form in the way in which we overcome gravity by standing upright. These spirits of form are to some extent the ruling forces in earthly existence, in our planet's present metamorphosis. But as we know, the spirits of form work through other spirits, for whom we use the old terms, yet in a modern, spiritual-scientific sense, of archai, archangeloi and angeloi.

Our first, immediate concern is with the archai, the primal or archetypal forces, or primal origins. We know that in the hierarchies of spiritual beings the spirits of form come directly above the archai. In the innate stream of our evolution, which I have drawn as white in the picture here (see diagrams pp.77–78), the archai forces have served the spirits of form. Within our human nature and being, the archai and exusiai—or spirits of form—are at work, the spirits we call the primal forces or origins. In addition, though, are particular spirits of form who disguise themselves as archai. These ought by nature to be exusiai, but do not work as such, choosing instead to manifest as archai. It is important for us to understand and penetrate this fact: within the active structure of the universe are beings who have disguised themselves, who apppear to stand at a different level of evolution from the one they actually belong to.

This has a very particular consequence. All that lives and exists as earthly form can be just as dependent on these spirits of form disguised as primal forces as it is on the actual spirits of form. It is important to remember that everything in earthly existence which connects with space by developing a spatial form arises out of a non-spatial realm. We only properly grasp what is spatial by tracing its image back to primal, non-spatial archetypes. It is very difficult, of course, for western thinking to imagine anything of a non-spatial character. Yet everything interwoven with our innate, archetypal humanity, which arises through spirits of form by taking shape in the realm of space, is in fact the effect and result of the non-spatial. To give a concrete example of this: each one of us starts off on all fours, a crawling baby, then learns to stand upright, overcoming gravity in our upright posture, placing ourselves into space. The force, though, which enables us to do this, is one which streams out of non-spatial into spatial realms. If we were subject only to the spirits of form belonging to us, we would in all possible ways, in all our relationship to the spatial realm, manifest the non-spatial within space. The spirits of form do not inhabit space. The divine cannot be sought in space. The spatial forms and shapes which evolve, derive from and are a realization of the non-spatial realm.

Those beings, then, who are really spirits of form but act as archai, belong essentially to this non-spatial realm. Yet they enter space, are active within it. And the fact that they do this, that spiritual beings whose true nature resides in non-spatial realms have chosen to disguise themselves and be active within the spatial realm, is characteristic of ahrimanic tendencies. The result of this is that forms arise in space which do not stream in from non-spatial dimensions. What is spatial, in other words, gives rise to other spatial forms, one just reflecting the other.

Let us make this more concrete. We human beings are all different from one another because we enter life out of the non-spatial realm. The archetype of each one of us resides outside of and beyond the spatial realm. Nothing in this world is exactly the same as anything else. You may know the famous story of Leibniz' experiment.[5] He asked some princesses (who often seem to have nothing much to do!) to search a garden for two completely identical leaves. They didn't find them, of course, for no two things are completely alike. We all share this characteristic of forms arising out of the non-spatial, inasmuch as we are different from one another. But there are ways in which we are alike—specifically through blood relationship—and such similarity is due to those spiritual beings who form the spatial in accordance with the spatial, rather than from the non-spatial. We resemble each other as a result of ahrimanic forces which permeate us. We must look this fact in the eyes, otherwise we will have a merely negative attitude to the influence of ahrimanic and luciferic forces without wanting to really understand them.

This example illustrates very clearly how Ahriman plays

into our life. We are part of the innate human stream of evolution to the extent that we recognize ourselves as individuals, different from each other. If this was the only force at work within us, if the ahrimanic stream did not play into things, no mother could rejoice that her little daughter resembles her so very closely, for she would be imbued with a sense that each individual is a spatial reflection from a non-spatial realm, and no spatial form can resemble any other. The fact that certain spirits of form do enter into space gives the ahrimanic an opportunity. The ahrimanic tendency is, of course, not limited to physical resemblence between people, but extends to many other things. This was just one example.

Now I would like you to recall what I mentioned in passing, not to console you particularly, but because it was part and parcel of the theme, after saying that we only really become ripe for self-knowledge in the second half of our lives.[6] To the extent to which our life takes its course through time without any other form of influence, we would indeed never attain self-knowledge until we had reached middle age. But, as I then said, luciferic forces work upon us in the first half of our lives and give rise to a self-knowledge that is not the result of our own innate, original human nature. Against this original stream of evolution I set what I called the *enduring* realm. Everything belonging to our original human nature looks quite different when we are 50 from how it did when we were 20. We develop, evolve. Everything in us that does not evolve or develop, which belongs not to the physical but to the soul and spirit, is connected with the enduring realm, in which time plays no part. Just as the non-spatial underlies and gives rise to the spatial, so the enduring realm is the foundation of all that is temporal and circumscribed in time.

We would be quite different people if we were not connected to the enduring realm. We would then, as I said before, not begin to wake up and stop dreaming our way through life until the age of 28 or 29. Our connection to this realm enables the balance of our lives to be somewhat redressed, so that we do not simply doze through the first half of life and turn into terribly bright sparks in the second.

Now to this enduring realm belong all the spiritual beings of the higher hierarchies with the single exception of the exusiai. These play into the realm of temporal evolution. Their existence passes between spatial and non-spatial, gives rise to a shaping and forming from the non-spatial into spatial realms. This process is subject to time since their activity enters temporal existence. But the other, higher beings, belong to the enduring realm alone. We cannot speak of them as temporal beings at all. Of course it is hard to try to describe these things, for nowadays only very few people can activate a real sense for non-spatial and non-temporal concepts. Most people would regard ideas about what is timeless, non-spatial, imperishable—even immutable—as pure fantasy.

Above the exusiai, then, there exist only beings who belong to the enduring realm. But among these are ones who disguise themselves as temporal beings and enter into time. Like the ahrimanic beings who enter into space, there are beings who enter time, and these are luciferic. They are beings who really belong to the spirits of wisdom, but assume the guise of the spirits of form because they work in time. And what would otherwise work timelessly in human souls during life, is brought down into the temporal realm by these spirits. So certain things which would always be available to us if we were allowed to keep our sights on the enduring realm, succumb to the temporal; are forgotten, for instance, or only partially remembered, which is due to our body-soul nature, not to our soul-spirit constitution.

Spirits of the enduring realm, therefore, who assume the guise of spirits of time, are luciferic. They are actually very high beings, of a much higher rank than those to whom many clergymen, however theologically elevated they may think themselves, refer to as the divine. The 'divine realm' of many clergymen is of a much lower order than these luciferic beings I am speaking of.

These luciferic beings are able to transpose into time what would otherwise appear to us as purely spiritual and timeless; they give it the appearance of temporality. This temporal semblance, with which certain phenomena in ourselves are endowed, is the sole reason why people maintain that their spiritual activity has a material, physical foundation and origin. If our souls were not penetrated and permeated by luciferic beings, our spiritual activity would appear to us in the pure, unmediated form of spirit. We should never imagine that spiritual activity could depend on matter. We would become aware that the only fitting image—one I often use—for the belief that our spiritual activity arises from matter is that of a person standing in front of a mirror who believes that his reflection comes from an entity behind it. The image does, of course, depend on the way the mirror is constructed; in the same way, our thinking depends on our physical nature. The body, though, plays no greater role than the mirror. Human beings would have a direct perception of this were it not for the luciferic illusion that spiritual activity derives from matter. To the degree to which Lucifer takes part in our surconscious, he conjures up in us the illusion which deceives us as surely as someone is deceived who breaks a mirror in order to try to reach the 'entity' behind it.

This illusion, of the spiritual arising out of matter, is essentially a luciferic one. And whoever subscribes to it is really making Lucifer into his god, though he may not admit as much.

We can also look at the opposite pole or position. If it is a luciferic deception to imagine that the mirror of matter causes a spiritual emanation to arise, it is ahrimanic to think that the things of the sense-world could have some influence on the human being's inner soul. Were it not for this ahrimanic illusion, which arises as a result of powers which enter the spatial realm from the non-spatial, we would clearly see that the forces rooted in the material world can never actually exert an influence over our inmost being. It is entirely ahrimanic to assert that there are forces and energies rooted in matter which permeate the human soul; whoever believes this makes Ahriman into his god, even if he does not admit as much.

Yet we swing, oscillate between these two poles, these two illusions: firstly, the luciferic—that the mirror itself produces pictures of real beings, in other words that matter could give rise to spiritual activity by itself; and the other, the ahrimanic—that within the outer sense-world are contained energies which can somehow be metamorphosed into inner human activity.

Our present time is characterized by its disinclination to investigate the spiritual with the same energy and focus that it directs towards the natural world. It is, of course, easier to speak about the spirit in a nebulous way, or in abstract terms, than to investigate spiritual processes and impulses in a truly scientific manner. But we now live in an age in which we must begin to become aware of what is at work in our souls. We know the reason for this, why the time is now past when we could draw from an unconscious source the impulses we needed to guide us. We have to make inroads into the realm in which our soul nature dwells, from which our conscious awareness arises.

We can say, therefore, that we would be very different beings indeed if our sole path of evolution was the one we were originally endowed with, and if we were open only to the good spiritual influences—if, in other words, the temporal luciferic and ahrimanic forces did not accompany our own archetypal direction and development. But how can we establish equilibrium between these three directions? To start to answer this question we must consider the following.

External science is actually rather sloppy in certain of its methods. It acts according to principles which are not much different from thinking that we might as well get out a razor and lay it ready by the plate, to use for eating! Many scientific conclusions are not much more sensible than that—ideas about death are one example: modern science does not ponder it more deeply than to describe it as the cessation of an organism. That conveniently allows many who call themselves researchers to talk in a rather grotesque way about plant death, animal death and human death all in the same breath. But that is not really any different from putting a table-knife and a razor in the same category. What can be called death is, in fact, a quite different phenomeon in each of the three realms. But people like to generalize, taking into account only the common denominator, a cessation of organic function.

When we study human death, which we have often spoken of, we can discover in it something of a counterbalance to luciferic forces. Death, as you know, is not a single isolated phenomenon; we begin to die the moment we are born. The impulses of death are laid in us from the beginning and eventually manifest in actual death. These impulses within us provide a counterbalance to luciferic forces, for it is death which leads us out of temporality into the enduring realm.

Now we know that the luciferic forces really belong by nature to this enduring realm, that they transpose into temporality the activity they are supposed to carry out in the sphere of timelessness. This dislocation would have no opposition if death, which leads us from the temporal to the enduring realm, were not placed into the realm of time, as a doorway. Death balances and counteracts luciferic influences: these carry eternity into time, while death bears time back into eternity. These are abstract words, yet they contain an enormous amount of specific, concrete reality.

And Ahriman? He is responsible for similarity—I have given you a concrete example of this in facial similarity between human beings. Against this influence, too, a counterpoise must be activated. But, strange to relate, the counterbalance to ahrimanic similarity is something which our muddled conceptions, failing to see the deeper context, normally identify *with* it—the forces of heredity. We are not alike merely in the shaping of our outward form, but we also bear forces of heredity within us. These forces actually work against similarity of form—only a confused and superficial science identifies similarity with heredity. We look like our parents, but at the same time we have certain forces within us which we inherit from them, which strive to reunite us with the original archetypal image of the human being. Such forces actually combat similarity, and we can see this at work if we try to observe life with more care and subtlety, not by using any supersensible powers but just through precise external perception. If you try to put the right questions to life, try to observe people who have inherited a particular outward feature from their parents, grandparents etc., you will find that their inherited moral impulses usually work against similarity of outward appearance.

Just think of various famous historical personalities who closely resembled their forefathers: you will almost invariably find that in the course of their lives they come to express soul qualities, actually as a result of hereditary forces, which are quite opposite to the inherited characteristics of outer appearance. This is one of the mysteries of life. Understanding of one generation for the next, of parents for their children, would be far better if people could recognize this fact. If a mother has a little son who is very like her, there is no reason why she shouldn't be pleased. But to develop the same inner qualities as well may not be desirable at all—especially the ones, for instance, which make for rows and quarrels between her husband and herself. We should take a very close look at actual instances and specific impulses at work in people, which are of huge significance for life. They are particularly important in the field of education—we will urgently need to be aware of them, to understand them in the future, for the sake of the whole future of human evolution. In the future people will not be able to educate their children by means of abstract principles but will have to seek out the empirical, actual basis and foundation for educating. And this will not be possible unless they learn to read the book of life—and before they can do this, they will need to 'learn their letters'. There are, of course, far more than just three 'letters'; but this ABC will do for the immediate future: normal evolution, ahrimanic evolution and luciferic evolution. Only by learning to read life, by applying a knowledge of these basic letters, will the unreal Utopian spirit so widespread these days be overcome. People instead will have to embark on a study of the actual forces at work in life.

Someone may well object that the archetypal nature of the human being I have referred to throughout is something that no one has ever discovered. That is true, of course, but it is like saying that I cannot see any oxygen or hydrogen in the river water flowing in front of me. We have to investigate these things, above all develop a proper conception of the nature of form. I have in the past used the following metaphor, which I would like to remind you of:

Whether in Coblenz or Basel, or elsewhere, you can come upon the Rhine, and wonder maybe how old it is—this river that's been flowing for centuries at least, perhaps since time immemorial. But what do we mean by old? What is actually old about the Rhine? The water you see there will have gone elsewhere in a few days time, and a few days ago it was somewhere quite different, so the water itself is not old. And you probably don't mean, either, just the channel the water has made in the earth. You actually mean something that cannot be seen. In the same way, when you speak of truth you cannot really refer to what is in front of you, for it is a confluence, a mingling of streams of reality flowing through the world, in a state of relative balance. Everywhere you look you see only confluence and relative equilibrium, and to find reality you must penetrate into the phenomena before you. Only by doing this can you develop a knowledge of the alphabet you need in order to be able to read the book of life.

Tomorrow I shall speak about the connection of luciferic and ahrimanic impulses with the Christ-Jahve impulse, so that you can begin to see the relationship of the latter to these two streams.

III. THE ‘FALL’: CONSEQUENCES AND COUNTERBALANCE

1. The Midgard Snake, the Fenris Wolf and Hel

Members of this audience who wish to subject my lecture of yesterday to philosophical scrutiny[1] might meet with apparent difficulties. They will have heard in the course of previous talks on similar themes that the purpose of our entire post-Atlantean epoch, and even of the later stage of Atlantean evolution, was gradually to develop the human ego and bring it to fuller consciousness. I have said that the people of the ancient Indian civilization, who had been able in Atlantis to perceive the worlds of spirit by means of the old clairvoyance still widespread then, were more or less the first to experience a direct transition from such clairvoyant perception to consciousness of the physical world. The whole of the post-Atlantean world reacted to this physical realm as one of Maya or illusion, while still experiencing the world of spirit as true reality. I pointed out in my last lecture, and the facts confirm this, that the people of this ancient Indian civilization had undergone a rich soul development, that they had attained a high stage of evolution while their ego was still more or less asleep; they had, in other words, only woken to ego-consciousness after their souls had attained a high degree of maturity.

The Indian peoples must therefore have had a quite different experience of their soul-development than the people of Europe, particularly the Germanic people, whose ego-consciousness was awake at the same time that their capacities were gradually evolving, and who were conscious of the divine, spiritual power working into their souls. You may find it difficult to reconcile this, at least in philosophical terms, with what I said yesterday. For those of a philosophical turn of mind I must add something in parenthesis by way of explanation.

The apparent contradiction resolves itself at once if you remember that perception of the ego is quite different from any other perception or cognition. When you perceive and recognize any object or being other than the ego, two aspects are involved: the person who is involved in the act of recognition, who applies the power of cognition, and the thing which is perceived. It doesn't matter, in terms of the pure straightforward act of cognition, whether what is recognized is a person, an animal, a tree or a stone. But it is a different matter when the ego perceives and recognizes itself, for then the knower and the known are one—subject and object of cognition are the same. It is important to realize that in the course of human evolution, as individual consciousness develops, these two things become distinct from each other. Those who had been part of the rich maturation of Indian culture in the post-Atlantean period developed the ego as a subjective experience of knowledge; this subjective enhancement of the ego within the human soul may exist for a long time before the human being acquires the power to see the ego objectively, as a separate entity. The European peoples on the other hand, developed this power relatively soon while still preserving the old clairvoyance; in their clairvoyant field of vision, in other words, they perceived the ego as a being among other beings. If you distinguish carefully between these two modes of perception, any philosophical difficulties will be resolved. If one takes pleasure in philosophical formulations one could express it like this: the Indian culture represents a soul nature which reached the full flowering of the subjective ego long before an objective perception of the ego developed. The Teutonic peoples, in contrast, developed a perception of the ego long before they became conscious of their actual inner ego impulses. Clairvoyantly, in imaginative picturing, they saw the dawning of their ego long after they had been used to perceiving the ego objectively in the astral world around them as one among other beings. We must clearly distinguish between these two divergent states, then we will also understand why Europe in particular was destined to associate this human ego with the other, higher beings, the angels and archangels, in the way I described yesterday in relation to mythology.

If you bear this in mind, you will realize that Europe was destined to relate the ego in a multiplicity of ways to the sense-perceptible world, and that the ego, our inner being and essence, can enter into the most varied relationship with the external world. Before the human being was conscious of his ego, before he perceived it, these relationships were determined for him by higher beings while he himself remained a passive instrument. His relationship to the external world was a purely instinctual one. The decisive factor in the ego's development is that it should progressively determine its own relationship to the external world. The task of the European nations was in large part to determine and form this relationship of the ego to the whole world. The guiding folk soul of this region had and still has the task of directing Europeans in this endeavour—bringing their ego into relationship with the outer world, with other egos and with the world of spiritual beings. This is why it was on the whole within European culture that people first started to speak of the relationship of the human ego to the surrounding universe. The atmosphere prevailing in old Indian cosmology is therefore quite different from that of the mythologies of Europe. In the East everything seems more impersonal; above all the attitude towards knowledge is passive—the ego is suppressed in order to merge with Brahma and find atman within oneself. The primary objective is to shed one's identity and seek union with the Absolute. In Europe this human ego occupies a central, focal position, which accords with its original innate tendencies and its progressive development through the course of evolution. Here, therefore, particular attention is given to seeing everything in relationship to the ego, to developing clairvoyant perception of everything in earthly existence which has had a part in helping the ego to evolve.

Now you all know that two opposing forces have participated in our earthly evolution, through the course of which we were destined to acquire an ego. Ever since the Lemurian epoch,[2] luciferic forces have imprinted themselves on the inner human being, the astral body. You know that these forces made our inner life the focal point of their attack, by infiltrating our desires, impulses and passions. There were two consequences of this: we were able to become free, independent beings, to be fired with enthusiasm by what we think, feel and will, rather than continuing to be under the sway of divine, spiritual beings in all that directly concerns us. But as a result of these luciferic powers we also had to accept our potential for evil arising through our passions, emotions and desires. Lucifer is omnipresent in earthly life, finding his point of attack in the human soul, in the interplay of human astrality. In addition, wherever there are points of contact and interweaving between astral and ego, the ego too has been permeated by the luciferic power. So when we speak of Lucifer we are speaking of an influence that has thrust us deeper into material, sensory existence than would otherwise have been the case. Both the precious gift of freedom and the dangerous potential for evil are passed on to us by Lucifer.

But we also know that the intervention of these luciferic powers in the entire constitution of human nature enabled other powers to enter us later on. We would see the world quite differently if we had not fallen under the sway of Lucifer and other beings who follow in his wake, if we had not been obliged to submit to the influence of another power after we had opened ourselves to the invasion of luciferic forces. Ahriman approached us from without and penetrated into the broad sphere of the sense-world surrounding us. The ahrimanic influence is therefore a result of the luciferic: Lucifer takes possession of us from within, and we are as a result susceptible to attack from without by Ahriman.

A science of the spirit worthy of the name, that develops real understanding for actual facts, speaks of both luciferic and ahrimanic powers. It may well strike you as strange, then, that folk mythologies of different nations and cultures are by no means always aware of this dual influence. The religious ideas embodied in the Semitic tradition, for instance, expressed in the Old Testament, have no clear perception of this. Only a certain awareness of the luciferic influence can be found in this tradition—evidence for which is the Old Testament account of the Serpent, who is really none other than Lucifer. There are generally very few signs of awareness of the ahrimanic influence, which is known of only where people, in all ages, developed a science of the spirit. The Gospel writers had knowledge of this. When the Gospels were written, the word devil or 'demon' had been borrowed from the Greek (daimon), and was used in many places—but not in the story of Jesus' temptation, over which Ahriman presided, where the word Satan is used.[3] But who notices these distinctions between the terms applied in Mark and in Matthew? External religion takes no notice of such subtleties.

If we compare the cultures of India and Persia, the contrast and moment of transition between these two influences appears quite clearly. The Persians were more subject to ahrimanic influence than luciferic. It was they, in particular, who wrestled with the powers which give us an external, false picture of the world, which surround us with darkness through the external influence of the outer world. Ahriman is known in the Persian tradition as the opponent of good and the enemy of light. Why does he figure here? Because in the second post-Atlantean epoch people developed a perception of the external world. Remember that Zoroaster strove to reveal the sun spirit, the spirit of light. But in order to do so he was compelled to show that alongside light the world is also composed of the spirit of darkness which muddies and confuses our external perceptions. The Persians strove to conquer Ahriman and unite themselves with the great light-bearing powers and spirits. Their nature and constitution led them to act within the external realm of the outer world,

which is why they spoke of the ahuras or asuras. It was dangerous for them, in contrast, to look inwards, to delve into an inner realm where the luciferic powers are concealed. For this reason they also turned away from the beneficial powers to be found there and looked instead towards the outer world, seeing there the asuras of darkness in continual opposition with the asuras of light.

The Indians of this epoch pursued exactly the opposite course. They tried to raise themselves to higher spheres by inner contemplation. They sought salvation by uniting themselves with the forces of inner vision. It was dangerous, they felt, to look out into the external world where they might have to wrestle with Ahriman. They feared this outer world and regarded it as dangerous. Whereas the Persians avoided the devas, the Indians sought to find them and be active within their sphere of influence.[4] The Persians turned their back upon this sphere, in which the battle with Lucifer is continually fought.

Search as you will through the many different mythologies and world-views, the clearest, most profound awareness of the fact that there are two influences at work upon us is to be found in Teutonic mythology. Since the Nordic peoples were still clairvoyant, they really saw these two powers and took up a position midway between them. They could see that in the course of evolution certain powers had penetrated into our inner being, worked in from without upon the astral body. And because it was part of the Nordic peoples' destiny to develop the ego, to achieve emancipation and independence, they not only sensed evil in this influence, but also above all an impetus towards freedom. They felt, one might say, the rebellious element manifesting itself in these forces. They felt the presence of the luciferic element in forces which were still at that time helping to create the different races, giving people their external form and pigmentation, and making them into separate beings who could act independently in the world. The clairvoyance of these Nordic peoples showed them that

Lucifer's influence was primarily one towards freedom, enabling them to overcome a passive submission to random external powers, allowing them to develop a solid inner core and a capacity for acting independently. This luciferic influence was felt by Nordic peoples to be a beneficial one.

But they also began to realize that something else stemmed from this influence. Lucifer conceals himself behind the figure of Loki, who has a remarkable shifting, shimmering form.[5] Because they could directly perceive reality, they could see that ideas about human freedom and independence arise through Loki. But they also perceived that it was Loki's influence which dragged them down, which made their desires and actions, their whole being in fact, of a lower nature than it would have been if they had been influenced only by Odin and the Aesir. Please sense the dire and awesome grandeur of this Teutonic mythology. At that time there was an absolute conviction and true perception of things which will only gradually return to people's consciousness through the science of the spirit.

How, then, does the luciferic influence act? It penetrates into the astral body and is thus able to work upon all three 'bodies' of the human being—astral, etheric and physical. At the present time we cannot do more than give hints about this luciferic influence outside the confines of the Anthroposophical Society. But you will come to understand more and more clearly that this influence makes itself felt in three different ways: in the human being's astral, etheric and physical bodies. In the etheric it brings about impulses of falsehood and lying. Lies and falsehood are not confined to our inner, emotional life. Within the astral body, the vehicle of our inner life, the luciferic influence exerts itself in the form of selfishness. In the physical body, it causes illness and death—that will be easily understood by those who were present at my last series of lectures.[6] I should like to emphasize once again that the signs and symptoms of physical death are karmically connected with the luciferic influence. Let me recapitulate:

through Lucifer there arises selfishness in the astral body, lying and falsehood in the etheric body, and sickness and death in the physical body. All materialists of the present day will be greatly surprised to learn that the science of the spirit attributes sickness and death to a luciferic influence, though there is also a connection here with karma. The karmic effect of the luciferic influence is that we plunge deeper into corporeality than we would otherwise have done, and so sickness and death arise to redress the balance, to re-establish equilibrium.

So when the luciferic influence entered the human being, the physical, etheric and astral bodies became prey to sickness and death, lying, falsehood and selfishness. Material science nowadays looks on death as an identical phenomenon in plant, animal or human being.[7] It fails to realize that something that seems the same in all cases may have a variety of underlying causes. An animal's death is not of the same kind as a person's, even though it appears outwardly to be so. It would take me far too long to prove this epistemologically. I can only say that the scientific view of causality is sadly mistaken. Such mistakes, which arise through muddled thinking, can be encountered at every turn. Imagine someone who climbs on to a roof, falls down, is mortally injured, and is found dead. What would be more natural than to say: 'He fell down, was mortally injured, and died from his injuries.' But there might have been a quite different explanation. He might have had a stroke while he was on the roof, and been dead already when he fell down. His injuries would then not have been the cause of his death.

This is a very crude example, but scientists frequently make this kind of mistake. The external facts may be identical, but inner causes can still be completely different.

For now, then, I would ask you just to accept these results of the science of the spirit: that the luciferic influence creates selfishness in the astral body, lying and falsehood in the etheric body and sickness and death in the physical body.

How would Teutonic mythology have pictured this threefold influence, ascribed to Loki or Lucifer? It would have been in terms of Loki's three offspring. The first is the Midgard Snake, the embodiment of selfishness, arising from Lucifer's influence upon the astral body. The second is the falsehood with which our perception and understanding gets entangled. On the physical plane this equates with the things in our mind which do not properly correspond with the actual facts of the world—untruth and falsehood in other words. The Nordic peoples, who still lived more on the astral plane than us, perceived falsehood as astral beings. Their way of expressing all that darkened the light of truth, that gave an untrue perspective, was in terms of an animal entity: chiefly, here, the Fenris Wolf. This second animal represents Loki's influence on the etheric body, which allows us to deceive ourselves, to have incorrect thoughts about things, to have a false perspective about things in the external world. The wolf is the astral embodiment of lies and all the falsehood which emanates from inner impulse.

But here, at the point at which we enter into relationship with the outer world, is also the point of contact between Lucifer and Ahriman; here error, illusion and maya infiltrate our knowledge, even clairvoyant knowledge, as the consequence of our tendency towards falsehood. The Fenris Wolf embodies the illusions surrounding us, our failure to perceive the truth of things. Whenever the ancient Teutonic peoples experienced a darkening of the light of truth, they embodied it as a wolf. This permeates the whole of Nordic consciousness. It is even applied to external phenomena. When these ancient people wished to explain what they saw during an eclipse of the sun—clairvoyance gave them a quite different perspective on things from the one we are familiar with through our telescopes—they used the image of a wolf pursuing the sun, who causes an eclipse by overtaking it.[8] This has a close inner connection with the outer facts. Such terminology is integral to the melancholy grandeur peculiar to Teutonic mythology. I

can only mention these things in passing—I could speak for weeks on end about them and you would then see the far-reaching inner consistency of this whole mythological world. That is because it arose through old clairvoyant faculties into which ego-consciousness had penetrated.

Our modern materialists will reply that this is pure unfounded superstition, that there was no wolf in pursuit of the sun. But that would be a failure to understand that ancient Nordic people saw the facts of the outer world in imaginative pictures. This image—the wolf and the sun—is actually far closer to the truth than many so-called scientific truths, which are infiltrated by a great deal of Ahrimanic influence, and consequently error. The idea that an eclipse occurs because the moon comes between the earth and the sun, actually seems to the occultist to be a view based on superstition. This explanation is true as far as external phenomena are concerned, just as the wolf and sun image is true from an astral point of view. The astral view, though, is in some ways more correct, more embracing of the truth, than the one you will find in all modern text-books. I realize this will seem absurd to contemporary minds. But in anthroposophical circles we are, I believe, now capable of understanding how our physical perception of the world is most influenced by maya, deception or illusion.

Let us now turn to Loki's influence on the physical body.  His third offspring is Hel, through whom sickness and death come about. Hel, the Fenris Wolf and the Midgard Snake are wonderful embodiments, dream-clairvoyant, astral perceptions, of Loki's or Lucifer's influence. If we were to examine the Loki story in every detail, we would find that everything illuminates and confirms our understanding of these things. We must be quite clear that clairvoyant perception does not produce allegory, but has vision of actual beings. The Nordic  peoples were not only aware of Loki and the luciferic influence, but also of the polar opposite influence of Ahriman. They knew, as well, that being entrapped in the ahrimanic

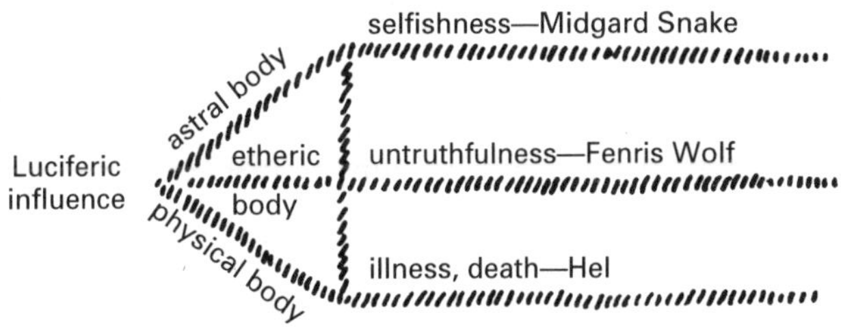

influence was a consequence of the luciferic influence. If you now look back to the time when people did not apprehend the world through sensory perception, but contemplated it through ancient clairvoyant powers, you will find a myth that actually describes and corresponds with these powers. What does it say? That human beings succumbed to Loki's influence, expressed in the Midgard Snake, the Fenris Wolf and Hel. The result of this was that their perception, their clear, luminous vision into the spiritual world, became dimmed. At this period people had an alternating consciousness between vision of the world of spirit and awareness of the physical plane, just as we alternate between waking and sleep. When a person of those ancient times gazed into the spiritual world, he looked back into the world from which he had been born. The mythology of that time—this is the essential point—had its source in clairvoyant consciousness, but there was still a continual alternation between insight into and loss of insight into the world of spirit. In the dreamlike, clairvoyant condition, people perceived the spiritual world; in the waking condition they were blind to it. This alternation was expressed in the mythological imagery of the blind Hödur on the one hand, and the clairvoyant Baldur on the other. If it were not for Loki, people would have developed in harmony with Baldur's influence. It was because of Loki that the blind Hödur-nature overcame the clairvoyant Baldur-nature. This is expressed in the story in which Loki provides Hödur with the mistletoe which he uses to kill Baldur.

Loki/Lucifer therefore drives the human being into the

arms of Ahriman. Our submission to the blind Hödur, and the slaying of Baldur,[9] is one and the same thing as the extinction of old clairvoyant vision. The Nordic people felt that the death of Baldur rendered them powerless to revive their former clairvoyance. This enormously important historical process, the gradual loss of the old, unclouded knowledge, is expressed in these stories: Loki and his three aspects of influence on the one hand and the tragic slaying of Baldur on the other.

So Teutonic mythology gives us a very clear reflection of knowledge we can also derive from the science of the spirit: the twofold influences of Lucifer and Ahriman. It would take us beyond the scope of this lecture to pursue this subject further now. But even in the broad outline I have described, you can feel something of the awesome grandeur of this mythology—unsurpassed, because no other myth so precisely embodies the process of dimming clairvoyant powers. Greek mythology is more a memory of something experienced in earlier times, expressed in almost sculptural form.[10] It does not have that immediate, direct involvement with contemporary condions which we find in Teutonic mythology, but is more sophisticated and mature. The figures and characters are more clearly defined in a sculptural kind of way, and the simplicity of direct, immediate experience has been lost.

In the North, then, the old powers of clairvoyance which had long since vanished throughout the rest of Europe were retained for a while.[11] There had been a gradual process of dimming perception until at last the physical world became the only perceived reality. At the time that Christianity began to spread, the truths depicted in the myth of Baldur had become reality for the majority of people, but in the North a direct perception of the spiritual world survived; and because it was so immediate, sprang so directly from real experience, it stood its ground for a while as Christianity began to spread and take hold. The northern peoples still had a feeling that their experience of a divine home and origin was vanishing, but it was not until it had truly vanished that they could receive the consolations of Christianity. Yet Christianity could not offer them any direct vision. They had experienced the tragic fate of Baldur far too deeply to be consoled by this God who had descended to the physical plane so that people who could only perceive this plane might rise again to divine consciousness. Unlike the people of the Near East, the Northern peoples were unable to respond to the words: ‘Change your attitude of soul, for the Kingdom of Heaven is at hand’.[12] In the Near East, where Christ appeared, there were only ancient memories of a time of clairvoyant consciousness. The Kali Yuga, the age of darkness in which people could no longer perceive the world of spirit, had already lasted for three thousand years. Yet they had still always longed for this world, and retained the traditions in which old memories were preserved. That is why they were very open indeed to the words: ‘Change your attitude of soul, for the Kingdom of heaven is at hand’. They could understand the profound words of John the Baptist: ‘The Kingdom of Heaven has come close, come down to the physical plane; therefore look upon the One who will appear in Palestine. Look upon the Messiah whom the God indwells, through whom you will once more be able to establish a connection with the divine, even though you cannot raise yourselves above the physical plane. Recognize the One who appears in Palestine, the figure of Christ.’

The Nordic peoples felt this differently. They had been embedded for far longer in actual vision of the spiritual world. So instead there arose in them other thoughts of very great, far-reaching importance: that this confining of perception to the outer physical realm, this darkening of spiritual vision, would be only temporary, an intermediate stage; that there would be a period of trial and probation during which they would have to acquaint themselves with the physical world and learn what it had to teach them. This was a necessary transition, a training period, they recognized, which required

them to withdraw from the spiritual world. But they would, by passing through this probation in the external world, find their way back again to the world they had lost sight of. The vision of Baldur would one day once more reappear and ensoul them. The powerful idea, then, that arose in the course of Teutonic evolution, that those worlds would once more reappear which had vanished from sight, gave these people the sense that their enforced period within the phyical plane was only a transitional one.

Their initiates taught them that changes were taking place in the spiritual worlds during this transitional period, and that these worlds would one day appear again, but transformed for their vision. They explained this by saying, more or less, that the beings they had seen previously in divine realms—the archangel of speech, runes and breath, Odin; and the angel of egohood, Thor—would no longer appear in the same guise.[13] It would, they said, be possible for those who prepare themselves in the right way to re-enter the spiritual world, but when they did they would find that other powers had joined the old ones, and the configurations and interrelationships between the gods would be different.

These initiates described the nature of the future vision that people would have who once more regained perception of the spiritual worlds. They described what would come about through the conflict of Lucifer with the gods, and how this would run its course. They gave their people an image of the Twilight of the Gods or Ragnarok. And we shall find that the imagery they employed, all the tiniest details of the processes at work, could not have been better portrayed than it was in this wonderful story. The Twilight of the Gods is a precise, accurate description of underlying occult truths.

So how should we see ourselves? We should recognize that all that stems from earlier times lies within us as an impetus for further evolution. We should be aware of what we have received as a gift from Odin, but also that we then passed through a subsequent process of evolution. We should grasp hold inwardly of the teachings which Odin planted in us, seeing him as an archangel figure. We should become sons of Odin and enter the battle, enter it soon. The initiate, the leader of an esoteric school, makes this clear to his pupils, especially those in Northern lands,* by pointing them to the divine, spirit being who appears in such mysterious guise, who really only comes into his own at the Twilight of the Gods, because he overcomes the power which originally overcame Odin. The avenger of Odin assumes a very decisive role in the Twilight of the Gods. If we can understand this role, it will reveal to us the wonderful connection between the natural disposition of the northern Teutonic people and our vision of the future. All this is expressed in a wonderful way, down to the very last detail, in the mighty vision of the Twilight of the Gods.

---

* This lecture was given in Oslo (transl.).

2. The Tree of Life, and the Tree of the Knowledge of Good and Evil

We saw yesterday that there are two cultural streams, two tendencies flowing through the course of history: on the one hand that of developing knowledge and wisdom; on the other the life-forces which at a certain point must unite themselves with this wisdom.[1] This is one example of the way in which different one-sided tendencies produce harmony and wholeness when they unite and work together—a fact whose consequences are really of earth-shaking proportions. So we can perceive the after-effect of a lifeless, dried-up and sclerotic wisdom; and see how the unknowing, untutored life-principle, like a green shoot on the branch of human evolution, unites itself with this primordial, withered principle of knowledge and wisdom.

Today I would like to examine this objective fact from a more intimate and subjective point of view, by looking more closely and directly at our human nature. Let us first recall, as so many times before, how we pass every day through a rhythmic alternation between the unity of our four 'bodies'—physical, etheric, astral and ego—and a condition in which these four are to some extent separated into two and two, so that the physical and etheric remain united with each other but are divided from the other unity of astral and ego.

The alternation between sleeping and waking depends upon this rhythmic uniting and separating of the four bodies. We have already looked at this process in greater depth.[2] Even without passing through any particular stages of schooling, people can have a real sense at the moment of waking, that very clear, very illumined moment, that they lift themselves, draw themselves up out of an immersion in the interweaving, rarefied waters of spiritual life.

Most people must sometimes have sensed this; must, on waking, have felt that they were not emerging from oblivion but from a far more ethereal interplay of forces than they usually inhabit during their waking lives. Many people, surely, will have noticed that they dwell during sleep in an element which allows them to be cleverer than they manage to be during the day. There can be few who have not at some time or another woken with the realization that they have encountered something during sleep that they cannot clearly integrate into their waking consciousness. This experience can make us feel rather thick-witted in contrast to the clarity vouchsafed to us in sleep's weaving, ethereal life. During sleep we are immersed in a world of weaving life-forces, that surround us in a way similar to that in which physical life interweaves its fabric with our physical consciousness, and which is usually wholly forgotten at the moment of waking.

Even without an occult schooling we can realize that during sleep we are immersed in an element that we cannot wholly transpose into our waking lives. We can understand why this is by recalling the primal duality we spoke of yesterday: human beings have learnt to distinguish between good and bad, they have eaten from the tree of knowledge of good and evil and for that reason they cannot eat from the tree of life.

What does 'not eating from the tree of life' mean? To understand this, we also have to understand what resulted from the fact that we *did* eat from the tree of knowledge of good and evil. Everyone can realize that if the so-called luciferic temptation had not happened, we would live on earth in a quite different way. The temptation of Lucifer has had a specific effect on human life; as a result of it we can develop a particular kind of knowledge and reason, a particular way of relating through our powers of reason to things around us. This kind of relationship to the world and its phenomena arose because of Lucifer's temptation and influence, because we tasted the fruit of the tree of knowledge of good and evil. All our knowledge is a result of this. If we had refrained from tasting this fruit our knowledge would be of a quite different kind to what we think of as 'normal' in the Lucifer-influenced conditions we exist within today.

Please hold on to this fact—that all the knowledge of our waking consciousness is a consequence of our eating from the tree of knowledge. You will then find it more comprehensible when I tell you another fact, one based on many occult perceptions, that our nightly, sleeping unknowingness, the unfolding of the dark cloak of sleep over our consciousness, is simply the effect of not being allowed to eat from the tree of life. Just as our daylight knowledge is the effect of having tasted the fruit of knowledge of good and evil, so our unknowingness during sleep results from not having been allowed to taste the fruit of the tree of life. If we had been allowed to eat this fruit our consciousness would not be dulled, darkened during sleep.

But when we overcome this condition of unconsciousness during sleep, when we become able, through systematic spiritual-scientific self-development, to perceive something of the reality of that ethereal interplay of forces I spoke of, then we become aware also of *how* we spend the time between falling asleep and waking up again. This may shock us, for we actually spend this time in the arms of Lucifer. And this fact can open our eyes to the whole, mysterious, underlying context; for we perceive that at the same moment that we were punished by being forbidden to eat from the tree of life, Lucifer was condemned to eat continually from it. So this interweaving, ethereal life that Lucifer inhabits and that we experience, on waking, to be imbued with intelligence beyond our own, that we cannot perceive consciously because Lucifer has claimed it as his own, has a quite specific effect.

Because Lucifer has appropriated this realm of interweaving, ethereal life, something does *not* happen that should actually have belonged to our destiny, that the divine Yahveh beings predestined us for. It was intended that on waking we should receive into our etheric and physical bodies the ethereal fabric woven during sleep.[3] Let me draw this for you, in schematic form. Here is the ego-aspect (*red*) that dwells outside the physical body during sleep; this (*yellow*) is the astral-aspect, that also leaves the physical body; here (*blue*) is the physical body that remains in the bed; and here (*yellow ochre*) is the etheric body that also remains behind.

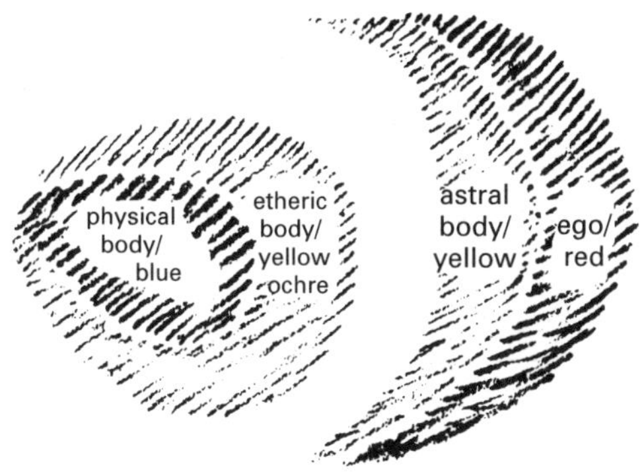

The evolving Yahveh deities preordained that on waking, the ethereal, weaving life I spoke of should descend into the human being's etheric and physical bodies. Don't let it scare you that Lucifer is interwoven with us when we are immersed in the ethereal interplay of forces during sleep. In my Munich lectures[4] I pointed out that it would be quite wrong to think one should try to keep out of Lucifer's clutches at all costs. That is actually a materialistic prejudice. Spiritual entities exist for a reason. There is no point in trying to deny or repudiate their existence. What we should do instead is recognize the validity and purpose of Lucifer and Ahriman *within their proper element*, and learn to see that they are only harmful where they do not belong. It is right and proper that Lucifer lives and weaves in our sleep-life, within the element that is closed to us because we have a different knowledge, which we gained by eating the fruit of the tree of knowledge of good and evil.

But there is a necessary process of evolution which the

science of the spirit now makes possible, which we should begin to understand, and which the moment of waking can allow us to perceive. The subtle after-effect that we can be aware of on waking, of the weaving life we are immersed in during sleep, should penetrate our physical and etheric bodies. This weaving ethereality is actually our astral body, that lives in the waves and currents of the cosmic ocean. And the tapestry it weaves there, the experiences it interweaves with, should enter and penetrate both our etheric and physical bodies.

Let me try to draw this, to depict the original intentions of the Yahveh divinities guiding human evolution, who preordained that all that our astral body passes through in the night should be integrated with our etheric and physical bodies (yellow diagonal lines in drawing a)

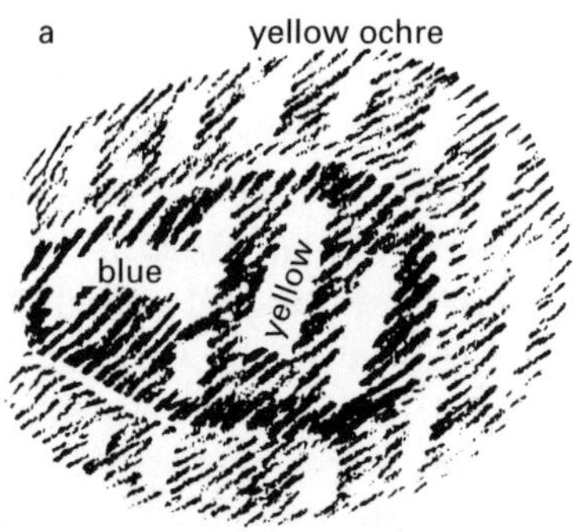

What I have drawn here represents the inhalation, as it were, by our etheric and physical bodies at the moment of waking, of all the experiences of our astral body. This should have come about during our human earth-evolution (or our earthly human evolution) if the original intentions of the Yahveh deities had been fulfilled. The luciferic temptation prevented this. Something else came about instead, which we must draw differently.

Here, in schematic form of course, is the physical body

(*blue*) and the etheric body (*yellow ochre*). The experiences of our astral body during sleep only penetrate the etheric body at the moment of waking. They may leave a faint impression in the physical body, influence it subtly, but nothing more. The only real penetration is of the etheric body.

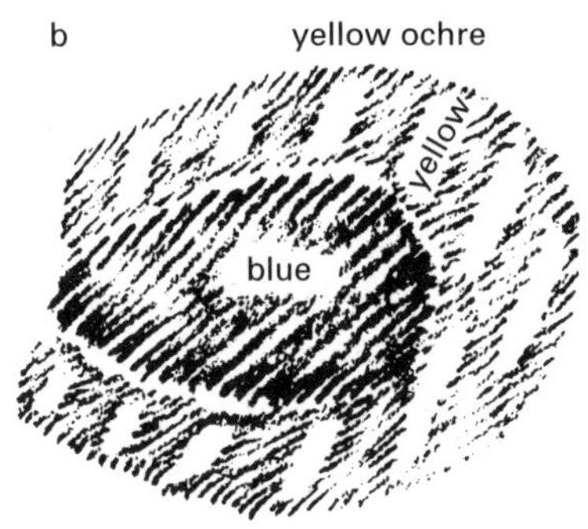

This is not because the astral body is held back, not because the physical body opposes it, but because of a mysterious pact between Lucifer and Ahriman which came about through the interweaving of luciferic and ahrimanic evolution with our earthly evolution. The result of this is that at the moment of waking, Lucifer passes to Ahriman all that ought to penetrate the physical body. The conditions that should exist, the astral weaving depicted here in drawing a, do not penetrate our physical body but instead are passed to Ahriman dwelling there. The ahrimanic process is drawn here as yellow points interspersing the blue diagonals. So we are faced with a very significant fact. Ahriman, in our physical body, receives the experiences which Lucifer has during our sleep. This is why we fail to integrate our night-experiences into waking consciousness. Lucifer passes them over to Ahriman as we wake up. But as they sign their deal each night, make their pact anew, we can become partially aware in our ordinary dreaming state of what passes hands between Lucifer and Ahriman. Now let us consider the ordinary everyday kind of

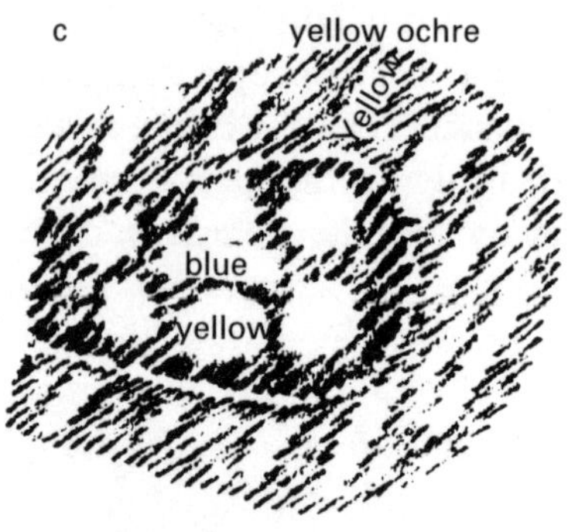

knowledge we have between waking up and falling asleep. This kind of knowledge, you remember, is the result of us having eaten the fruit of the tree of knowledge of good and evil. During the day we gather knowledge of the things around us, a knowledge which combines our reason and intellect with our sense-perceptions. This human, earthly knowledge, as you no doubt realize, comes to us via our ego, is vouchsafed us by virtue of the fact that the ego has been added during earthly evolution to the three other principles we brought over from previous Saturn, Sun and Moon stages. As earthly human beings we gain through the ego human knowledge—that is, we learn all that is possible for us under the conditions which we inhabit here on earth. But this kind of knowledge is characterized by the fact that it grows dim and dark the moment we fall asleep.

So we gather knowledge from dawn to dusk as it were; but when we fall asleep this knowledge stops being consciously available to us. In other words it leaves our ego. Philosophers who make the ego the sole foundation of their approach, and believe this is tenable, who regard the ego as a constant factor between birth and death, are talking nonsense. Our ego, at least our conscious experience of it, is extinguished every night. So let us be clear: we gain and gather knowledge through the ego, but this ego is extinguished every night between falling asleep and waking up again.

Why is this so? Our 'daylight knowledge' is gathered in the realm which Ahriman has appropriated. Ahriman's kingdom is our external, physical reality—because he presides over all death, because death is his 'property' as it were. I went into this in detail in my Munich lectures.[5] Our consciousness traverses Ahriman's realm between waking and falling asleep once more; the normal, everyday kind of knowledge we develop, as a result of the luciferic temptation, leads us during our waking life into the domain of Ahriman. We dwell under Ahriman's dominion in our orientation towards outer knowledge which relates to the external world of the senses.

Lucifer led us into this state of affairs; but—we must make a clear distinction here—we do not dwell in Lucifer's realm in our waking life, but in the kingdom of Ahriman. It is hard for us to realize this, since Ahriman inhabits our physical body. He is always there, ready to help when we desire to acquire knowledge through the medium of the physical body, through the senses. He squats in us, and Lucifer hands over to him the 'takings' of the night, all that he experiences in us while we are asleep. During the day, in conjunction with Ahriman, we acquire our worldly knowledge. When we fall asleep, Ahriman pays off the score to Lucifer, more than rewarding him for what he, Ahriman, received when we awoke. He gives to Lucifer when we fall asleep all that he experienced in us through the day. The effect of this is that what should happen does not. All that we live through during the day ought to be transposed on to our experiences at night, like this (drawing a, green); but in fact reaches only as far as the astral level, as Lucifer takes receipt of it in the ego (drawing b, small circles). While we are asleep, Lucifer in us experiences all that resonates and works on in us from the day-time knowledge we acquired while awake. So we can say that Ahriman, not us, enjoys the fruits of our night experiences; while Lucifer, in our place, enjoys the fruits of our day-time experiences at night, within our ego. Ahriman within our physical body, Lucifer within our ego; Ahriman during the day, Lucifer during the night.

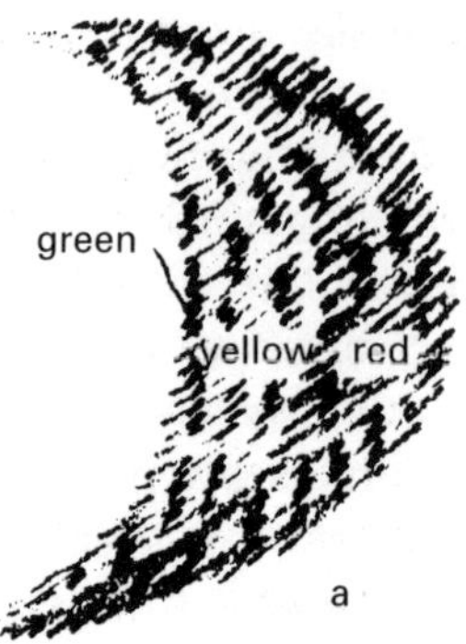

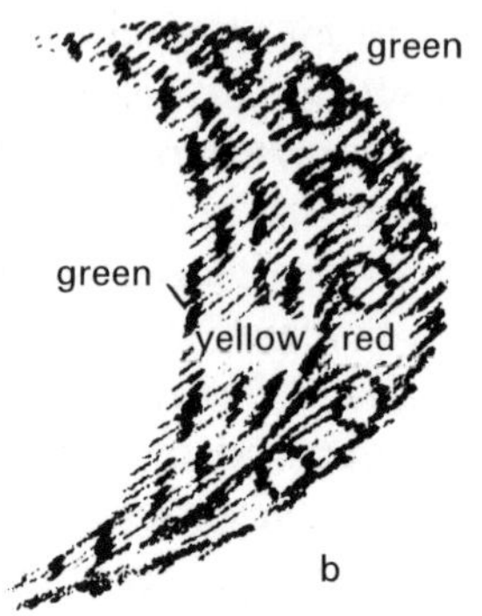

What we have to do is become aware of the consequences of this state of affairs. Let's look first at what is going on while Lucifer occupies our ego during the night. This actually prevents us from fathoming or re-experiencing at night all that we acquired during the day, all that we thought and judged about the world, all our interconnections and ideas about it. If we could continue this process at night, we would really penetrate these daytime experiences.

The Yahveh deities originally intended that the knowledge we acquired during the day should be permeated and penetrated by us at night. If this had happened, our knowledge and science would have been of a quite different kind—a much more vital and living science, in which each concept of ours would really live within us. We would also be aware that the concepts we experience during the day are the shadows of living beings, as I have often described.[6] During the night we would perceive all the concepts we had formed during the day coming alive, waking up into the forms of elemental beings. We would know that the science and knowledge we developed was actually alive, was a real, living, weaving force within the world—active, elemental, weaving life.

But it cannot be this for us, for Lucifer grasps hold of it and deprives us of it. He takes living knowledge away from us. Every night he sucks dry the living content of our knowledge, leaving us only with the abstract, dry husks, the dead concepts which science provides.

This is why science is something we experience as incapable of drawing close to the vitality indwelling all things, why it seems to deal just in dead concepts about what lives and weaves as reality in the world. The scientific approach makes us feel that we are removed from life, that we stand outside it and cannot find the way in. All that philosophers have construed and conversed about since time immemorial about the limits to knowledge, about our human inability to penetrate the underlying depths of existence, has been due to the fact that they had some sense of whole realms of reality and life beneath the concepts we form. They had a sense that we cannot come close to these realms because Lucifer sucks their life dry, occupies them, thus rendering our concepts arid and abstract.

Now let us also look at the other side of the coin. What would happen if we were not subject to Ahriman on awaking, if he did not seize hold of all that we experience during the night? Our day-consciousness would then be filled, would resonate with all our nightly experiences. The whole spiritual world would enter into our waking consciousness, would mingle with it. Our present alternation between waking consciousness and night-experience would not be present in the same way at all. Our waking consciousness developed in the way it has through Lucifer. If he had not exerted the influence upon us which he has, our waking consciousness would have a quite different relationship to the things of the external world. In that case we would also be quite capable of accommodating the influx of our night experiences into waking consciousness. But we would then experience our waking life in a very different way.

In our daily life we observe the world around us, form ideas, concepts and images about all that surrounds us. We make connections, combine ideas and perceptions; yet between birth and death we are confined to just coupling together things we experience through waking consciousness. But if our night-experiences really entered and penetrated our waking state, we would be able to connect each day-experience with a memory of what we had passed through during sleep.

As things are now, when we meet someone whom we know, we are only aware of this because we have encountered him as part of our waking experiences. We connect our present meeting in waking consciousness with a past meeting of the same kind. But it would be quite different if our night experiences penetrated our waking life. We would then know that the person we meet corresponds with a particular being of spirit whom we encounter at night. We would have experienced him during the night and would be able to identify him with his spirit entity and context. We would perceive the spiritual interweaving his physical appearance. The whole world would, in this condition, become clear, spirit-interwoven reality. But the luciferic temptation has prevented this. The spiritual aspect of life is withdrawn from us—Ahriman grasps hold of it, and we are left only with its presence in our etheric body (see drawing b, page 120). It sits there in our etheric body and does not penetrate us fully, so we fail to perceive its reality in the things around us. We can sense the streaming, weaving life of the spirit through our etheric body—we can have a general sense of it—but do not manage to integrate it with our external perceptions.[7]

I hope you can follow me: instead of the spirit entering the physical body, so that it is present in all our specific perceptions, it stays put in generality. So we feel that the spirit is there, that it indwells the world, but it does not reveal itself to us in concrete and specific ways. Above all it cannot inform our external knowledge and science. It could only do this if it penetrated the physical body; it remains no more than belief because it is experienced only through the etheric body.

So the fact that many people reject specific knowledge, preferring belief, is due to the fact that they have a quite correct sense that such concretization could lead to error, that they would rather remain embedded in 'normal' life. Belief is actually knowledge that has got stuck in the etheric body, whereas the knowledge we acquire by day gets stuck in the astral body by night, and so grows lifeless. Living belief, devoid of real knowledge because Ahriman has appropriated it, is the counterpart to the knowledge without belief, the knowledge from which Lucifer has extracted belief. Here, in this drawing (last drawing b, page 120) we can also see that Lucifer in our ego undergoes ahrimanic experiences.

Let me sum up, in the hope that these very important observations will lodge in your memory. Ahriman and Lucifer are intimately involved in our lives; they work together, preventing us from establishing a proper harmony and equilibrium between belief and knowledge. Instead we oscillate between the false poles of unknowing belief and unbelieving knowledge.

But it is quite false to think that we could ever escape the clutches of Lucifer or Ahriman. They have their cosmic task—all that has happened had to happen. Humanity, as I described yesterday, had to descend the path of gradually dying knowledge, as expressed in the condition depicted here (drawing c, page 118). And in contrast to this, against the flow of this stream, there arose in Central Europe a type of humanity which evolved this other tendency (drawing b, page 117). Only the confluence, the harmonizing, of these two cultural streams will allow a living realization, a real implementation of the Christ Impulse to take place.

But it is also possible that these two streams will diverge, will take separate courses in their understanding of Christ, will wholly lose sight of what they have to offer each other. Let us just assume for a moment that this European stream falls prey to Ahriman, is overcome by the power Ahriman exerts over waking consciousness. Let us assume that this stream then expanded and strove for an understanding of the Mystery of Golgotha: it would tend to reject the external context, the outer fact and Event of this Mystery, for it would not desire to thread the needle of the physical body, to penetrate it fully. Overpowered by Ahriman, it would draw back from a real and concrete grasp of this mighty, cosmic Event of Christ's Descent. Instead, it would inhabit the inner world and approach Jesus through the human etheric body, founding a Jesuology, a theology and knowledge of Jesus. It would therefore reject all that reaches out into the outer world from the Mystery of Golgotha, all that penetrates external reality.

If, on the other hand, the condition depicted in this drawing (drawing b) gained the upper hand, there would be little interest in our inner connection with the human being within Christ, with Jesus. Far more attention would be paid, dictated by the nature of this tendency, to a broad, abstract understanding of cosmic workings. This stream strives to develop a Christology, as opposed to the Jesuology of the first. But truth resides in the equilibrium between, in perceiving the unity of Jesus Christ and Christ Jesus. This is the aim of the science of the spirit. It does not wish to come down on one side or the other, but to be clear both that Christ is a cosmic Being—who first resided beyond the earthly sphere, then entered it through the Mystery of Golgotha, who thus gave the whole of human evolution a quite new Impulse, who brought down from the cosmos into earthly conditions something which flows on, working upon them and transforming them—and that at the same time there is a deep inner connection between these Events and the man Jesus of Nazareth. We must realize, in other words, that Christ, as He was before the Mystery of Golgotha, could not have penetrated the earth with this cosmic event without the physical, human body of Jesus; that he therefore *had* to pass through the Mystery of Golgotha. It was necessary for Christ to experience what he experienced in Jesus.

Neither Jesus alone nor Christ alone, but Christ in Jesus. This is the unity we need. What happened on the earth did not take place through Christ alone, but through Christ indwelling Jesus. A pure Christology is as impossible as a pure Jesuology. The science of the spirit can get nowhere without Christ Jesus. The fact of the Mystery of Golgotha is intrinsic to what was needed for our earthly evolution.

If the destiny initiated by the Mystery of Golgotha is to be fulfilled so that a right, balanced relationship can be established between Lucifer and Ahriman in regard to all that human beings make happen in the world, then we must recognize and understand how Lucifer and Ahriman work together within us. We must consciously oppose their hand-in-hand operations. We can do this by pursuing a science of the spirit that characterizes these two tendencies as clearly as possible, and allows us to find a way through to Christ.

This is what I sought to express in the wooden sculpture that is to occupy a central position within our new building.[8] The archetype of the human being in the centre, between the powers of Ahriman and Lucifer. Here, in immediate, artistic form, is depicted something which reaches forward into our evolutionary future, which in a sense replaces with a new Trinity the ancient Trinity belonging to the past: Christ—Lucifer—Ahriman. We will speak more of this next time.

IV. THE INTENSIFICATION OF EVIL AND THE TASK OF OUR PRESENT CONSCIOUSNESS SOUL AGE

1. Supersensible Aspects of Historical Research

Even within the limits which discretion still dictates at the present time when speaking of such things, we cannot discuss the Mystery of evil without profound emotion. We touch here upon one of the deepest mysteries of the fifth post-Atlantean epoch, something which most people's capacity for understanding and feeling is not yet evolved enough to grasp. Yet in all so-called secret societies of recent centuries, repeated efforts have been made in imaginative and symbolic form to illumine this Mystery of evil and the closely related Mystery of death. But since the last third of the nineteenth century, these symbolic representations have either been dispensed in a rather flippant manner, in Masonic communities for instance, or have been treated in the way I spoke about nearly two years ago, when I was talking about important events of the present time.[1]

What I said at that time was not without a deeper motive; whoever knows something about these things is aware what unplumbed depths of human nature we touch upon here. But there is ample evidence of the general lack of will for understanding what is involved. Such determination to understand will come, though, and we must ensure that it does so by every means at our command. In speaking of these things it will sometimes seem as though some form of criticism of contemporary life is intended. What I said yesterday, for instance, about the world-views and perceptions of the bourgeoisie, chiefly since the last third of the nineteenth century, but also really for much longer than that—can, taken superficially, be seen as criticism.[2] Yet criticism is not intended. What I wish to do is describe and characterize, to trace the forces and impulses which have been influential. From a certain point of view we can see that these impulses were necessary—it is possible to show the historical necessity of the fact that the bourgeoisie of Europe slept away the decades between the forties and seventies of the last century. But that does not mean that we should not now be clear that this cultural sleep occurred; our awareness of it can have a positive effect, can awaken in us certain impulses of will and understanding that work on into the future.

Two Mysteries—as I said, I can of course only speak of these things within certain constraints—are of quite particular importance for our evolution during this period of the consciousness soul, which started at the beginning of the fifteenth century. These are the Mysteries of death and evil. The first, that of death, certain of whose aspects must in our time be seen in connection with the second, evil, immediately raises the vital question: how does death relate to human evolution?

I have said before that what passes for science in our times takes the line of least resistance in these matters. For most scientists, death is simply the cessation of life, irrespective of whether we are talking about a plant, animal or human being. The science of the spirit, in contrast, cannot go down the easy road of reducing everything to its common denominator—otherwise we would end up being unable to make a distinction between the death of a person and the demise of a pocket-watch. The death of human beings is quite different from the 'death' of other beings. We can only understand the phenomenon of death in the context of those forces at work in the universe which, when they get a hold of us, bring about our physical death. Certain forces and impulses are active in the universe, and if they did not exist we would not die. These forces are at work in the universe of which we are a part; they therefore work through us as well, and their activity in us brings about our death. But we must ask ourselves what else they accomplish besides our death. Our death is only a secondary effect and it would be wrong to imagine that that is their sole purpose. No one would dream of saying that the railway engine's function is to wear down the rails although that is one aspect of what happens. The engine does gradually wear away the rails—it cannot avoid doing so—but that is not its function and purpose. It is as nonsensical to say that a locomotive is designed for the purpose of wearing out the railway track as it would be to think that the forces in the universe which bring about our death exist for that sole purpose. Their real, primary function is to endow us with the capacity for developing the consciousness soul.

From this you can see the intimate connection between the Mystery of death and the fifth post-Atlantean epoch, and how important it is that in this epoch the Mystery of death should be generally recognized by all. The forces which as a secondary effect cause our death are really destined to implant, to inject into our evolution not the consciousness soul itself but the capacity to develop the consciousness soul.

By understanding this you not only gain insight into the Mystery of death but your power to think clearly and precisely about important matters is also honed and sharpened. Contemporary thinking—and again I am not criticizing but describing—is in many respects simply sloppy, if you will excuse the expression. Modern thinking, especially in the science of our day, is almost entirely of the 'train-existing-to-wear-down-the-rails' variety. This sort of thinking is plainly inadequate for the task of creating a healthy future for humanity. In the age of the consciousness soul such a future can only be achieved in full consciousness.

We should not for a moment lose sight of this fact, which is a truth of profound importance for our times. You often hear of people who seem to have some inner fund of wisdom upon the basis of which they make suggestions for the improvement of social or economic life. But no really valid improvements to our condition—and only those whose thinking accords with the times will understand this—can come from any other source than the science of the spirit; all other pronouncements about future social forms are pure quackery. People who look to the learned pedantry of political economists, whose knowledge is devoid of spirit, are sleeping through the real needs of their age.

The forces, then, which must be described as forces of death, took possession of our corporeal nature in much earlier times already—how, you can read in my book *Occult Science*.[3] Only now are they penetrating the human soul. For the remainder of our earthly evolution we must assimilate these death-forces, and in the course of the present epoch they will develop in us the capacity for bringing the consciousness soul to full expression in ourselves.

In the same methodical way in which we examine the Mystery of death and see in it an expression of forces at work throughout the whole universe, so we can also examine the forces at work in the Mystery of evil. These forces are also not ones which primarily aim to bring about human evil. If forces of death did not exist in the universe, we could not evolve the consciousness soul. Our further evolution could not assimilate the powers of the spirit-self, life-spirit and spirit-man.[4] We must pass through the consciousness soul stage if we wish to take into ourselves the powers of the spirit-self, life-spirit and spirit-man. For this to happen we must wholly unite our being with the forces of death during the fifth post-Atlantean epoch, that is, up to the middle of the fourth millennium. This lies within our power. But we cannot unite with the forces of evil in the same way. Their nature is such that we will only be able to assimilate them, as we now assimilate the forces of death, during the Jupiter period. The forces of evil, one can say, work upon us with less intensity, taking possession only of a portion of our being. To understand them we must turn away from their outer manifestation and effect, and search for evil where it reveals itself most truly, where it manifests in cosmic forces working upon and entering into ourselves.

At this point we touch on something that can only be spoken of with deep emotion, something that can only be uttered in the full confidence that it will be greeted with the most profound seriousness. If we wish to trace evil in the human being we cannot seek it in the evil actions and deeds committed in human society, but in the propensities, the tendencies towards evil. We must first look right away from the results of such propensities, which manifest more in some people and less in others, and turn our enquiring gaze upon the underlying tendencies, asking ourselves in whom the propensity for evil manifests during our fifth post-Atlantean epoch, in whom a tendency for evil dwells—whose outer, secondary effect comes to expression so clearly in actual evil deeds.

The answer to this question can begin to dawn on us when we try to pass the Guardian of the Threshold, as he is known, and really come to a true understanding of our human nature. The answer then grows clear: since the beginning of the fifth post-Atlantean epoch, the propensity, the tendency for evil lies in the subconscious of *every* person. It is this very influx of evil propensities into human beings that marks our entrance into the fifth post-Atlantean epoch. Expressed radically though quite correctly, we can become aware by crossing the threshold to the spiritual world that there is no crime, however dreadful, that we as people of the fifth post-Atlantean epoch do not have the propensity for. Whether this tendency actually leads to a crime or evil action in an individual case depends upon wholly different circumstances, not upon the propensity itself. So you see that if we are to tell humanity the plain unvarnished truth we cannot escape uncomfortable facts.

Once this realization has dawned in us, the question becomes still more insistent about the purpose of these evil-inducing forces in us. What on earth is the reason for these forces in the universe which infiltrate our being? They are certainly not there *in order* to bring about evil acts in human society. They no more exist to provoke us to criminal actions than the forces of death exist to make us die; they are present in the universe so as to awaken in us a propensity, once the consciousness soul has developed, for opening ourselves to the life of spirit in the way I described to you yesterday and on a previous occasion.

These forces of evil are active in the universe. We must assimilate them, and by so doing we implant in our being the seed which enables us to have conscious experience of the spirit. In the context of our social order they appear in a perverted form, but they really do not exist to incite us to evil acts. They exist to enable people at the stage of the consciousness soul to break through to the life of spirit. If we did not take up into ourselves these propensities for evil, we would not be able to consciously develop the impulse that opens us to the spirit coming towards us from the wide reaches of the universe, which must fertilize all cultural life if it is not to decay and die. Our best course is first to examine the evolutionary potential of these forces, which appear to us in perverted, caricatured form in human acts of evil, and ask where they may lead us as we develop further.

We can't, as you see, speak about such things without touching the living nerve of human evolution. They are closely related to the calamities that presently afflict humanity.[5] Such calamities, and others still to come, are no more than the first ominous signs, like the rumblings of distant thunder, of what is to come—rumblings which still, in our times, often give an impression quite different from what they actually herald. These things are not said to cast down your spirits, but to provide an awakening impulse for action. Not pessimism but rousing wakefulness is needed.

Perhaps we shall best achieve our purpose if we take as our starting point an actual, concrete phenomenon. I spoke yesterday of an impulse of great importance for human evolution in the consciousness soul age: people's mutual interest in each other, concern for each other, must increase and grow stronger throughout the further course of earthly evolution. In particular it must increase in four specific ways. Firstly, as we evolve into the future we must learn to see our fellow human beings in a constantly developing, progressively different light. We have already passed through somewhat more than a fifth of the consciousness soul era, yet we still show little inclination to see other human beings as we will have to learn to see them before the end of the age of the consciousness soul, in the fourth millennium. People still disregard the most important aspect of others, have no real insight into other people. They have not yet really made use of what the arts have nurtured in them and drawn out of their souls throughout repeated incarnations. The history of the evolution of art can tell us a great deal—I have referred to this on several occasions. If, as I have urged in these lectures, one observes the real symptoms, it is undeniable that almost all forms and branches of art and artistic appreciation are presently in decline. All the artistic endeavours of the last few decades must give anyone who has a sense for these things the feeling that art is at a low ebb, has become decadent. But art's most important legacy to future human evolution is the insight and education it can offer into particular ways of understanding and taking hold of the future.

Every branch of culture has, of course, many ramifications, and so all kinds of secondary effects; but art by its very nature embodies something that leads to a deeper, more specific and actual knowledge of the human being. Whoever makes a thorough, intimate study of artistic form in painting and sculpture, or of the nature of the inner rhythms and movement, the inner pulse in music and poetry—and artists themselves often fail to do this in our times—will, if his experience of art is deep and inward enough, imbue himself with something which enables him to grasp and encompass the nature of the human being in inner, imaginative, sculptural form. This is what humanity must develop in the age of the consciousness soul—the capacity to grasp the human being in inner imagination. We have already discussed some aspects of this. If we look at the human head it points us back into the past. Just as dreams can be seen as memory and recapitulation of outer sense-experience, endowed as they are with the 'signature' of the sensory world, so those who have insight into reality can perceive everything in the external sense-world as an image of the spiritual. We must learn to perceive the spiritual archetype of the human being through its outer image and form. As we progress into the future, the human being will increasingly become clear and transparent to us: the form of the head, the way a person walks—all such things will provoke a different kind of inner involvement and interest than is generally in evidence today. For we will in future only be sure of knowing someone else, of connecting with his real ego, when we can develop this kind of imaginative grasp, when what we see with our physical eyes can give us the fundamental feeling that it relates to his spirit, his supersensible reality, in the same way that a picture painted on canvas relates to the reality it depicts. This fundamental feeling must evolve. We must learn not to regard the human being before us as just a bag and bundle of bones, muscles, blood etc., but as the living image of his eternal, spiritual, supersensible being, to the extent that we would not be sure of recognizing a person if sight of him did not awaken in us a perception of his eternal core. This is how we will perceive others. When we see images of what is eternal in human forms and movements, and everything associated with them, we shall respond with feelings either of inner warmth or coldness arising from a very intimate perception and knowledge of what is at work in those around us. Some people will make us feel warm, others cold. Those who evoke in us neither warmth nor cold will be the worst off. We will experience an inner response in the warmth ether permeating our etheric body—a reflection of the more intense interest and involvement which must develop between people. The second aspect will provoke even more paradoxical feelings in those contemporary people who do not have the slightest desire to accept such ideas. Yet perhaps in the not too distant future this antipathy will transform itself into powerful sympathy for what is part of rightful evolution. This second aspect is the quite different way in which people will understand each other. To attain this, the two millennia from now until the end of the fifth post-Atlantean epoch will not be enough. This process will extend into the sixth epoch as well, adding to the insight and knowledge of another's ego of which I just spoke, the capacity to feel and grasp another person's connection with the Third Hierarchy, his relationship with the angeloi, archangeloi and archai. This will develop through an increasing recognition of a changed response to language, to speech, from the kind we have nowadays. The evolution of speech has already passed its zenith, as I described to you in this autumn's lectures.[6] Speech has already become something abstract. At the present time, a wave of profound untruthfulness is sweeping through the world in the form of outer structures and legislation based on national language divisions. People no longer have an inner connection to language which would allow language to reveal to them the inner humanity it expresses.

I have quoted on various occasions an example which may serve as a first step towards understanding these things.[7] I mentioned it again in a public lecture which I gave in Zurich, because it is important to draw the public's attention to such matters; I pointed out that a surprise awaits us when we compare the articles of Herman Grimm on methodological approaches to history (deeply rooted as he was in nineteenth-century European culture), with those of Woodrow Wilson.[8] I carried out this comparative study with great thoroughness and was able to demonstrate that certain passages of Woodrow Wilson can be substituted for passages by Grimm, and vice versa, for the wording is almost identical. Yet there is nevertheless a radical difference between the two, which we can perceive when we read such passages without focusing primarily on their content—for the actual word-by-word content will, as humanity evolves, increasingly lose its central position. The difference between the two is this: in Grimm everything is the fruit of personal endeavour; he has wrestled with the passages—even those with which one may not agree—sentence by sentence, step by step. In Wilson on the other hand everything seems to be prompted, given to him, by his own inner 'daemon', which subconsciously possesses him. The important factor is not the apparent outer content but the source: in the one case at the surface of consciousness; in the other the daemonic promptings which rise into consciousness out of the subconscious. Wilson's writings are, one can say, to some degree the product of a kind of possession.

The words themselves are not the most telling thing. I always feel extremely melancholy when friends of our movement bring me articles by some priest or professor and say: 'Do look at this, it sounds quite anthroposophical!' Contemporary conditions make it quite feasible for a professor who perhaps dabbles in politics to write things which sound, on the face of it, taken at the level of words, to be in harmony with a true understanding of the needs of our time. But the literal words are not what matters, so much as the region of the soul from which they arise. It is important to discover the source behind the words. I do not speak here with the aim of formulating particular sentences, phrases and principles: what is important is the 'how', the way in which words are permeated with the force and impetus of the spirit. Whoever finds a verbal similarity between papers written by a priest or professor and what I have said here, without sensing that my words spring from a spiritual source and are penetrated by their spiritual origin and immersed in the whole context of an anthroposophical world-view, fails to distinguish between clever words and theories and descriptions rooted in spiritual reality.

Pointing out such things can, of course, give people an uncomfortable feeling—nowadays we are far more likely to go in the opposite direction and take things at face value. But it is more or less a duty to address these issues, uncomfortable though they are, when what is at stake are things of real importance, when one's aim is more than just to use words to soothe people's uneasiness, provide them with some kind of palliative or cultural sleeping-draught. If we are serious about what we think and say we should wake up to the consequences for the world of ignoring the danger of allowing a half-baked American professor to dictate the way the world should be organized. It is not easy to speak of realities nowadays, since many people seek comfortable, illusory options. But in matters which are of vital importance, which deeply concern or should concern people, it is necessary to speak the unvarnished truth.

We must learn to see *through* words. We must learn to grasp the inner gesture of speech rather than its outer form. Before this epoch lasting into the fourth millennium ends—although not all will be achieved by then—people will have learnt to listen to one another differently from the way they do now. They will perceive in the gestures of language an expression of the relationship of human beings to the Third Hierarchy, to the angels, archangels and archai, an expression of our connection, beyond earthly confines, with the supersensible and spiritual world.

In this way the human soul will be heard, will sound through the medium of language, and this will lead to quite different social and community forms. And the so-called forces of evil must be transformed to such an extent that people will be able to hear through a person's words to the soul expressed within them. When this happens people will have a powerful experience of 'speech-colour', through which international understanding beyond all barriers of language can arise. A particular sound will evoke the same sensation in the listener as perceiving the colour blue; another sound will evoke in us a sense of red. The 'temperature' we feel when looking at someone else will, when we hear his speech, become an experience of colour. We will be unable to avoid an intimate, inner experience of the qualities conveyed on the wings of human speech to human ears.

The third aspect is that we will develop an inner experience of the emotional impulses and configurations of other people.

Speech will reveal much of this to us, but not speech alone. When one person encounters another, he will sense through his own breathing the other's emotional patterns. In future times our breathing will adapt to and assimilate the feeling life of the people we encounter. Some people will cause our breathing to slow down, others will cause it to speed up, and the rate of our respiration will tell us what sort of person we have encountered. Just think what deep effects this will have on the way social communities interrelate, how closely intertwined human relationship will become! These things will take a long time to evolve. For breathing to adapt in this way, to root itself in human soul life, will take all of the sixth and some of the seventh post-Atlantean epoch. And by the seventh epoch, the fourth aspect of which I wish to speak will have just begun to come about. To the extent that they activate their will in communal life, people will—excuse the expression—have to digest one another. The sensations and inner experience they will have when either compelled or wishing to activate their will towards some aim in community life, will be the same as we experience nowadays in primitive form when we digest this or that kind of food. In the sphere of will, people will have to digest one another, will have to breathe one another in their feeling life, and sense the colours emanating from one another in the realm of mutual understanding through speech. They will come to know one another as ego-beings by learning to see through to the realities underlying each other and themselves.

But all these forces will be more inward, more related to the life of soul. They will only fully evolve in the course of the Jupiter, Venus and Vulcan epochs. Yet our evolution requires us to start already on this path, to begin to develop the first rudimentary spiritual qualities which can lead us in this direction. Our present time and its strangely cataclysmic developments is an expression of humanity's opposition to the necessary processes of evolution I have described. Mankind is rebelling against the need to develop, in future, inclusive and non-sectarian social impulses, by fanning the flames of nationalism throughout the world. Events of the present times are an expression of humanity's revolt against the course of evolution desired by divine powers, a polarization, a counter-reaction against what must come. We must gain insight into such things if we are to develop real understanding of the so-called Mystery of evil, which is really a secondary effect of things that need to integrate with the course of our human evolution. When a locomotive with a long journey before it hits a bad section of track, it may destroy the rails and grind to a halt. I have described to you some of the goals of human evolution, which it is part of the task of the consciousness-soul age to consciously recognize. But the rails on the first part of the track are pretty rough, and there are no better rails in immediate view, at least partly because very few people are making any real effort to replace them with better ones.

The science of the spirit, though, does not aim to be pessimistic, but to describe and show exactly where we have got to at present. It also requires us to lay aside, at least at certain solemn and celebratory moments, tendencies which are widespread and general. One of the things which makes it so hard to speak openly about these matters nowadays is the difficulty people have in laying aside ingrained attitudes and habits without immediately collapsing back into the pig-trough. Addressing the issues I have raised today touches on things which presently threaten to engulf humanity, and in the face of which a constant warning and awakening call is needed.

There are many things indeed which can be discussed only within certain constraints. As a result, of course, I cannot address some issues at all, or must defer them for a future occasion. Let us take an example that closely concerns us—please do not take it amiss if I present it in the following way. A week ago I was asked to say something about symptomatic events in Swiss history. I have thought about this very carefully from all sorts of angles, but if I as a foreigner were to embark on a commentary about Swiss history from the fifteenth century to the present day, in the presence of Swiss people here in Dornach, I would find myself in a strange sort of situation. Let me first explain what I mean from a different standpoint. Suppose that in June of this year (1918), someone in Germany or even Austria had described the events and personalities involved in the current situation in the way everyone does now, only a few months later—just imagine what impression he would have made; and imagine also if this person had said such things five, or 15 or 30 years ago, predicting what would come about now! He would have got himself into deep waters! In the same way it is clear to me that I would cause great offence if I now spoke about Switzerland and Swiss history in a way that will actually be common in 20 years' time. For people cannot do otherwise, given their ingrained attitudes—please forgive me speaking so frankly—than close their ears to what the future compels us to recognize and express. People—among whom after all we must count ourselves—are in many respects unwilling to hear the truth spoken, especially in matters that concern them closely. They prefer to take a sleeping tablet or two. And I can assure you that I would cause offence if I did not just administer a sleeping tablet when speaking about the subject I have been asked to address. In the light of further reflection it seems best to me to leave this subject on one side for the time being. For judgements and perceptions which are current at the moment, with which I would have to differ, would have to be approached in the same kind of way that I did yesterday. Here in Switzerland it seems relatively harmless, not in the least threatening, to take a critical look at the Russian revolution and describe the relationship between the bourgeoisie and the broad masses, and more left-wing, radical elements. That may even seem like a better class of Sunday sermon—quite acceptable. One can even hope, perhaps not without some grounds, that some people will even pay more attention and ponder more deeply on such things than on a Sunday sermon—although my experience in the last few years has often taught me that the opposite is true where more important matters are concerned. But to subject something very close to home to scrutiny, to examine Swiss history before a Swiss audience from a non-Swiss perspective, as a foreigner, is asking rather too much. Even when I gave a general survey of modern historical developments, which I did recently in Zurich in a public lecture[9] and gave myself free rein, drawing the most radical, necessary conclusions, I still had to keep within certain constraints. For most people today are very comfortable in their appraisal of Woodrow Wilson as a great man, a benefactor of mankind. If one should deny this, should actually speak the truth, one will be regarded as a trouble-stirrer. This has always been the case for truths drawn from the sources of supersensible life. But we now live in the consciousness-soul age and it is necessary to make humanity aware of certain truths.

There is really no point in continually repeating the obvious—that people today are not receptive to things. The question is not about people's receptivity but about whether we ourselves do our utmost, given the opportunity, to make them aware of truths they need to hear. We should harbour no illusions; people nowadays are seldom receptive to the truths they most need to receive, just as they insist upon running the world in a way that is at odds with the true needs of humanity and the evolutionary impulse necessary to our time. One has to experience the bitterest disappointments in this regard. But one must accept these things without resentment and simply take them as an opportunity to learn how best to tackle each situation that arises.

I will speak in more detail about these things later. It would, you see, have been wonderful to have found even just a few members of the masonic tradition in Central Europe who could recognize the scope and importance of what I spoke about here two years ago, when I discussed the existence of certain secret societies.[10] But what I had to say fell upon deaf ears; for of course there has been nothing more sterile in recent decades than the position occupied by masonic tradition in Central Europe. This is illustrated by the resistance and opposition one encounters when refusing to amalgamate an anthroposophical science of the spirit with European Freemasonry. On the other hand, when a super windbag appears on the scene, the so-called Nietzsche specialist Horneffer,[11] and talks solemn nonsense about symbolism and the like, he is greeted in the broadest circles with enormous deference. The deeper reason for all this is that the science of the spirit makes certain by no means easy demands on those who wish to pursue it! Today there are advocates of spiritual renewal who tell people that they only need to lie down on a couch and relax, and the higher ego, God and heaven knows what else, will awaken in them. No need to wrestle with these awfully difficult anthroposophical concepts! Just listen to your inner voice, let yourself go, surrender passively—then the higher, mystical ego will manifest, and you will feel and experience the presence of God within!

I have known statesmen who prefer to listen to such views, so much easier than pursuing an anthroposophically orientated science of the spirit. A friend recently told me that one of these gurus had said to him, when he was still a disciple of his: 'You have no idea how stupid I am!' He said this no doubt to show that intelligence is not a necessary prerequisite for disseminating archetypal wisdom; he has a large following of people who agree with him! For many people much prefer to listen to such a message than suffer the discomfort of wrestling with all sorts of difficult stuff, such as the task of the consciousness-soul age, or a fourfold evolutionary path, or even that people should experience each other through a sense of warmth and colour, should breathe and digest each other. To get to grips with such things one might even have to read a whole pile of books—that would, of course, be dreadful! Yet the cataclysmic nature of our time is closely connected with the fact that people find these things too laborious and arduous to bother with. But there is still no cause for pessimism—these things instead are a call to activate our strength, to transform knowledge and understanding into action. This cannot be repeated too often.

Yesterday I illustrated what I had to say with the example of suction and pressure problems; and now I would like to leave you to ponder for yourselves whether considering such phenomena might not be very important. Not taking account of such things might tempt one to think that, whereas in Russia the bourgeoisie failed to find common ground with the peasants, here in Switzerland things will be different, the bourgeoisie and the peasants will join forces and socialism will make headway. But it's worth remembering that that is exactly what many people said in Russia, and that the fact that they said it has much to do with what happened there.

We will speak more of this tomorrow.

2. The Three Streams of Materialistic Civilization

The tasks facing mankind now and in the near future are decisive, far-reaching and important, and to get to grips with them to some degree will require strength and courage of soul. Looking at them in depth and endeavouring to reach an understanding of what is really needed today can prompt us to question the easy superficiality with which so-called public matters are dealt with nowadays, when politics appear quite random and haphazard. People form their opinions about life on the basis of a few emotional reactions, of views that are entirely personal or merely derive from their own particular cultural standpoint. Yet the seriousness of our present predicament would be better met by a desire to gain a proper foundation on which to base a truly sound judgement. I have spoken a great deal here about the demands which contemporary events make upon us, about the needs of our times,[1] always with the aim of enabling people to form their own opinions, and not to present them with ready-made views. The most important thing today is to have the will to fathom the realities of life with ever-increasing throughness, so as to acquire a true foundation on which to base one's judgements.

Far too few questions are asked about the really grave, actual facts. People who consider themselves to be extremely practical are actually the greatest theorizers, content with merely forming a few ideas about life to prop up their opinions. Yet only a thoroughgoing and all-embracing enquiry into life itself can provide a basis for practical assessment of what is really needed. To make politics at random or create wonderful theories about life without any grounding in reality is, to say the least, intellectually frivolous.

Our hope must be instead that people will develop a soul-grounded seriousness about life.

What we might call the practical side of our science of the spirit has most recently been offered to the world in the form of a threefold ordering of the social organism.[2] Yet the very way in which we have to think and formulate ideas so as to work out this threefold ordering is met with antipathy and prejudice. People have ready-made ideas about what the truth is, about what is good, right, practical and so on. Once formed, they assume these ideas have an absolute validity everywhere and for every age. A socialist in western or eastern Europe is likely to have certain quite specific socialist ideals, founded on the fundamental belief that because they satisfy him they will also satisfy all other human beings anywhere on the earth, and that they will remain eternally valid for all future ages.

Since people fail to understand that the underlying tenor and character of an age or place must dictate social ideals, they do not easily recognize how necessary it is to introduce the threefold ordering of social life into European culture and its American outpost in a variety of forms and nuances. As it adapts to a particular place and people, these variations and nuances will come about by themselves. The ideas themselves are not absolute; they are for our present time and the near future. But in order to assess the full importance of separating out within the social organism an independent cultural life, an independent life of rights and government, and an independent economic life, we must take a clear, unprejudiced look at the way these are intermingled in our European-cum-American culture. Our cultural life has a quite different origin from our life of rights and government, which, in turn, is a realm quite different and separate from our economic life. Yet these three strands of such differing origin are chaotically entangled. Today I want to trace the source of these three strands (see drawing, page 156).

A realistic, quite external assessment will find that we

assimilate our culture as an extension of the continuing influence upon us of the culture of ancient Greece and Rome. Graeco-Latin culture flowed on into what became our grammar schools and universities. Education in the humanities, right down to the primary school level, stems from the Greek element (orange in the drawing). Our European cultural life goes back to ancient Greece, Roman culture being simply a transitional stage. Of course, in more recent times this Greek culture has become interfused with mechanics and technology, commercial technology and so on. Besides the universities we now also have technical colleges, colleges of commerce and other such institutions which add a more modern element to what enters people's souls in the form of education—and not only the so-called 'educated' class; the socialist theories, for instance, that have so influenced proletarian thinking, are also merely adaptations of ideas already present in Greek minds and culture, which have passed through various metamorphoses.

This Greek cultural life which we find represented in Plato, Heraclitus, Pythagoras, Empedocles, and especially Anaxagoras, all originally derives from oriental culture. But it underwent a significant transformation during its passage between the Orient and Greece. In the East this culture was far more spiritual, and flowed from what one might call the Mysteries of Spirit, or I could say the Mysteries of Light (drawing continues). Greek culture was filtered and diluted in comparison with the oriental culture and spiritual life from which it originated.

We have to go back into prehistoric times because the Mysteries of Light, or of Spirit, emerged from pre-history. Right back in the third, fourth, fifth, sixth, even seventh millennium before the Mystery of Golgotha, there were human beings throughout the civilized Asiatic world who had access to spiritual truths through their natural clairvoyant capacities, which were bound up with their blood and physical body. The whole population in general had these faculties.

But their atavistic clairvoyance gradually faded and grew increasingly decadent; this not only affected their cultural life but also their social forms and organization. Why? Because from the widespread mass of the earth's population there arose a particular kind of human being, at various places but particularly from a central point in Asia, with special faculties. These people still retained their atavistic clairvoyance, the secrets of the universe still arose in them in a type of dream-consciousness from their inner soul life; but in addition they also had what we would call the power of thought. They were the first human beings in whom wakeful intelligence began to dawn.[3]

This was a very telling social phenomenon. Those ancient people, embedded in dreamy visions of the secrets of the universe, saw the advent of another kind of person who, besides this sort of vision which they could understand, also possessed something beyond them—the power of thought. The Indians later regarded the Brahman caste as having descended from such people who united atavistic clairvoyance with thinking. As they moved southwards from the higher northern regions of Asia they came to be known as Aryans.[4]

The Mysteries of Spirit, or better still of Light, were founded by people who combined atavistic clairvoyance with the first kindling of the light of inner, individual intelligence, a final outcome of which is our present cultural life. This shining spark of intelligence continued on as an after-effect into our own cultural life, but was no more than a residue. Much of what was then revealed has been preserved within mankind. But we must not forget that the decline and extinguishing of the old atavistic clairvoyance and its replacement by the power of thinking was already experienced in ancient Greece, particularly among the more educated populace. By Roman times only the power of thought remained. The Greeks had still known, though, that thinking arises from the same sources as their declining clairvoyance. That is why

Socrates could still speak of the *daemon*[5] inspiring him, even though this only gave him access to dialectical, intellectual truths.

The ancient Greeks also very tellingly showed in their art how the bearer of human intelligence stands out from the rest of humanity. A thorough study of Greek sculpture reveals three strongly differentiated types: the Aryan is shown in the head of Apollo, Pallas-Athene or Hera. Compare the ears of an Apollo with those of a Mercury and you will see the difference. In the Mercury type the Greeks wanted to show the merging with intelligence of the ancient, bygone clairvoyance that still lived on in the form of superstitious belief, and that this was a lower form of culture, an underlying foundation superseded by the Aryan Zeus-headed form. At the very lowest cultural level were the stages of ancient clairvoyant capacity, still present in Greece, and perceived by the Greeks to exist mainly at the geographical fringes of their country. This level was depicted in the Satyr type. Compare a Satyr nose or ears with those of a Mercury and you can see how the Greeks expressed awareness of their evolutionary path in their art.

What came through the Mysteries of Light or Spirit and was gradually filtered through ancient Greece until it arrived in modern times had the inner strength and influence to form the basis for that aspect of our lives to which laws and rights apply. On the one hand, then, is the divine revelation mediated through the Mysteries, bringing the spirit to human beings; on the other, the implanting of this spirit into the external forms of the social organism, into the theocracies. The theocracies were capable not only of administering the life of rights, the political and legal sphere, on the basis of the Mysteries, but could also regulate economic life by means of them. The priests of the Mysteries of Light were at the same time the economic and commercial administrators of their regions. They built houses, canals and bridges, and saw to the cultivation of the soil and so on.

The whole of this civilization was therefore originally founded on the impulses arising in cultural life; but these gradually became more and more abstract until they were nothing more than a collection of ideas. By the Middle Ages they had turned into theology—which is really just a compilation of concepts replacing the old living traditions of cultural and spiritual life. Because the connection with the spirit was lost, things had to be run in an abstract way by a court of justice. It is very hard to see, nowadays, that western rulers have inherited anything from ancient theocracies in which the king received his mandate from the gods, through the Mysteries. All that we are left with from those times are the outer insignia of crown and coronation robe. Everything which was once inner cultural impulse has become external rank and structure.

Hardly less externalized are the teachings that flow through our grammar schools and universities. These are a last echo of the messages received from the gods in the Mysteries. Spiritual and cultural life has become totally abstract, has, in the final analysis, become *ideology* such as is prevalent in socialist circles: a collection of thoughts that are just that and no more.

Today's social chaos has come about because a cultural life filtered and made abstract in this way loses all its strength and impetus. We need to set cultural life once more upon its own foundations so that it can start to flourish again. We must find the way from spirit that is nothing but outward thought, back to the source of creative spirit. Only a cultural life emancipated from political and legal controls and influence can flourish and grow strong. A spiritual and cultural life gagged by the Church or preserved and protected under the auspices of the state, or staggering under the burden of economic factors, cannot become fruitful for mankind. Only a free and independent spiritual life of culture can do so.

It is high time for us to find the courage in ourselves to state clearly and openly what we believe in: that cultural and spiritual life must stand on its own feet. Many people are nowadays asking what is to be done to remedy the ills afflicting contemporary life. The first thing to be done is to help as many people as possible understand that cultural life must be independent, must stand upon its own strength and impulse; that the nineteenth-century form of education in primary and secondary schools is no longer of any use, and that a new kind of education must arise out of an emancipated life of spirit and culture. People still have too little inner courage to stand up and be counted, to make known their demand for radical change. Such demands can only be made once enough work has been done to give as many people as possible the necessary insights into the nature of contemporary needs. Spreading clarity about these things, creating insight in people with every means at our disposal, is what we should be doing. Only by making cultural life free and independent from other factors can our culture start to flourish, become vital and productive.

All things that arise in the world leave traces behind them once they have faded again. The Mysteries of Light are still present in today's oriental culture and spiritual life, and in a less filtered and clouded form than in the West. If we look closely at Hindu or oriental Buddhist traditions we can discern traces of the origins of our own cultural life—though in Asia these origins remained at an earlier stage of development. But we have become extremely unproductive, the source of our cultural life has become something of a stagnant pool. When news of the Mystery of Golgotha spread through the West, the Greek and Latin scholars found the concepts to comprehend it in oriental wisdom rather than in their own ideas. The West did not produce Christianity, it came from the East.

Another example: when people in English-speaking parts felt their own cultural life to be sterile and impoverished and began to long for new inspiration, the theosophists turned to the colonized Indians and sought from them the source for a renewal of theosophy.[6] There was no such fruitful source in their own tradition. There are many further examples which prove the barrenness of spiritual and cultural life in the West. And all such proof is also proof of the need to give spiritual, cultural life an independent existence within the threefold order of the social organism.

A second strand in the tangle is that of the workings of the state, the life of rights and the law. This is the scourge of our civilization: these processes involving learned judges on their benches, together with the jury, passing sentence and pronouncing on crimes and offences, these officials administering our civilized world with their red tape, to the despair of those who are thus administered. Everything we call jurisprudence or the state, and all the politics that arise out of this combination of law and government, belongs to this strand (see drawing, page 156, white). This (orange) is the strand of spiritual, cultural life. And this (white) is the strand of rights and the state.

How has this all come about? We can trace it back to the Mystery culture of ancient Egypt, which then passed through parts of southern Europe, and through the sober, unimaginative Roman character, where it united with an off-shoot of oriental culture to culminate in Catholic Christianity, or rather the Catholic Church. This Catholic Church is in itself a kind of jurisprudence, to put it in radical terms. From the separate dogmas right up to that mighty final reckoning known throughout the Middle Ages and beyond as the Last Judgement, the whole—very different—spiritual life of the orient was given an Egyptian slant by the Mysteries of Space, and more or less turned into a bench of world judges passing universal sentence and meting out universal punishments from on high to the sinners, and dividing the world into good and bad.

This is the second strand in the tangle we call civilization; it has not united in any organic way with the rest, as you can easily ascertain by visiting a university and attending a lecture about state law and then a theological lecture on canon law.

They fit hand in glove with each other but hardly relate to people's actual experience of life. These things have moulded human life though. Even in these late times, when their origins have been forgotten, they still structure the life of human souls. The life of rights later worked to make cultural and spiritual life abstract, and its outer forms became our social customs, habits and institutions.

The final social outcome of the decadent spiritual stream of the East is feudal aristocracy (see drawing). The aristocrat nowadays shows little sign of his origins in oriental, theocratic culture, having divested himself of all things spiritual. And the bourgeoisie (see drawing) is the last vestige of something that also evolved from ancient origins, passing through the Roman Church constitution, through theocratizing law, through legislative theocracy, becoming more worldly in the cities of the Middle Ages, and totally worldly in modern times. In their ultimate outcome all these spiritual streams and forces are well and truly mixed and tangled up in human beings.

There is a third strand as well. Where (see drawing, red) does it appear most characteristically to outer perception? In the customs of commerce and financial life. In Anglo-American traditions of the world of finance are to be found the most pronounced vestiges of something which originally had quite different forms—what I would like to call the Mysteries of the Earth. The Druid Mysteries were only one particular variety and type of these Mysteries. Those European tribes who were entirely ignorant and barbaric as far as the revelations of oriental wisdom were concerned, who knew nothing of the mysteries of Space, or of everything that later became Catholicism, who encountered and opposed the spread of Christianity, had a specific form of wisdom that was utterly physical.

Historical study of this cannot trace more than the last vestiges and remains of its customs and traditions, but these were a source of the national habits and customs of England and America. Such traditions and festivals were quite different from those of ancient Egypt, where the harvest was related to the stars. Here (red strand) the harvest itself was the festival. The highest festive points of the year were closely related to economic life.

Here in this third strand, then, an economic life springs up that has to evolve upwards in contrast to the life of rights and law that was received from above in Asia and gradually descended to earth. This economic life engulfed the cultural and rights streams of life to such an extent that, for example, one of the major festivals in honour of the gods used to take place at the time of the impregnation of the herds. There were other such festivals, all arising out of the economic life. In northern and central Russia, Sweden, Norway, or in territories that until recently were parts of Germany, in northern France, and in what is now Great Britain, existed populations which had a distinct economic civilization long before the spread of Christianity. The traces we can find there of old customs of law and cultural and religious life, all contain echoes of this ancient civilization based on economics. This economic life encounters everything that comes towards it from the other two streams. Its original customs and traditions of law were discarded as the influence of Roman law made itself felt, and its original traditions of cultural life were jettisoned as Greek culture flowed into it. At first, encountering these things, this economic stream stagnates and become sterile, but gradually it works its way through again, though only by overcoming a chaotic state of affairs through absorbing a cultural life and life of rights that does not belong to it, that comes from another source.

Look at Anglo-American cultural life today and you will see two starkly differing elements. Firstly, more than anywhere else in the world, you can notice the existence of 'secret societies', which exercise more influence than people realize. These societies are proud to be custodians of ancient Egyptian and oriental culture—but this has become so filtered and condensed that it now consists of nothing but symbols and

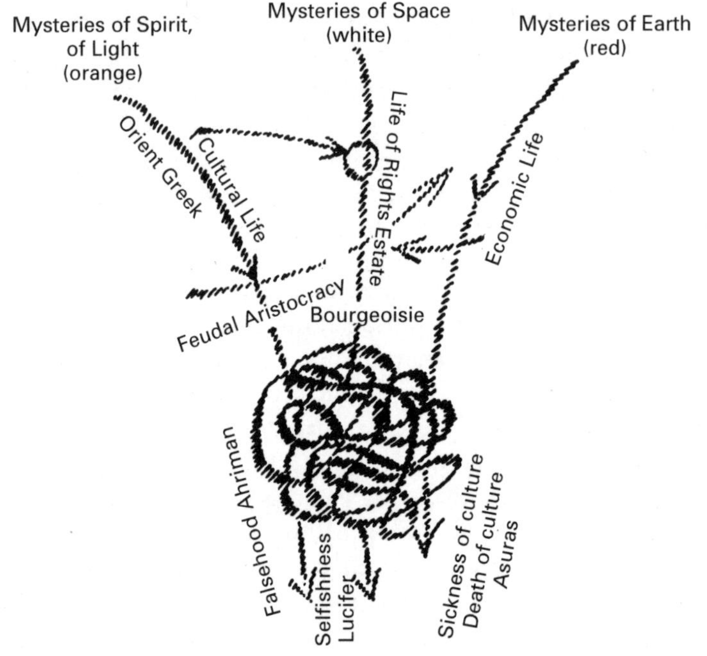

symbolic ritual that are hardly understood, though they secure great power for the leaders of these movements. But this is an ancient form of spiritual and cultural life, not one that has grown up out of the West's own soil.

The other aspect is a cultural life that is certainly grounded in the economic realm, but as yet has put forth only tiny flowers. Locke, Hume, Mill, Spencer, Darwin and others[7] are the tiny flowers sprouting from the soil of economic life. The ideas of a Spencer or a Mill are ones which flourish easily on such soil. Social democracy has then adopted them, elevated them into firm principles and tried to reduce cultural life to an appendage of the world of economics, believing that such things are derived from a practical approach to life, whereas in fact they reflect a fixed, routine way of thinking rather than any practice based on the realities of life.

On the one hand, then, we find such teachings as those of Darwin, Spencer, Mill and Hume; and on the other, the filtered and diluted Mystery teachings that flow on in various sects and movements such as the Theosophical Society, the Quakers, and so on. The economic life has as yet only pushed up a few buds and blossoms, while the cultural life and the life of rights remain alien plants—more and more alien the further west we go in European civilization.

In Europe there has always been a defensiveness, a kind of opposition to the alien cultural life of Greece on the one hand and the alien Roman Catholic life of rights on the other. Central European philosophy provides one example of this rebellion, though in England there is virtually no understanding for a Central European philosophical approach. It is actually not possible to translate Hegel into English. Nothing is known about him there. German philosophy is thought of as something quite foreign, with which sensible people can have no truck. Yet this German philosophy actually represents, in Fichte, Schelling and Hegel,[8] the late flowering of a rebellion against a transplanted, alien cultural life. Goethe also embodies the search for a free, emancipated life of culture and spirit, wishing to have nothing to do with the last echoes of Roman Catholic jurisprudence expressed in the 'laws' of nature. This term—'laws'—makes clear the ghostly presence which a legalistic approach still has within science. Goethe's science, in contrast, has to do solely with archetypal phenomena, with underlying specific conditions rather than 'natural laws'. This science of Goethe was in fact the first step towards a free and independent cultural, spiritual life.

Here in Central Europe the first step was also made towards an independent life of rights. Read Wilhelm Humboldt's essay *The Sphere and Duties of Government*,[9] and you will find a first attempt at constructing an independent life of rights or of the state, an endeavour to find independence for the political realm. Attempts like this, which began at the end of the eighteenth century, took shape in Central Europe. They were founded on important impulses which should not be ignored, for they too can lead over into a striving for ordering the social organism in a threefold way.

Right at the beginning of my book on Nietzsche[10] I quoted a sentence that gives us a sense of the tragedy afflicting German cultural life. In his essay on David Strauss, Nietzsche described the founding of the German Reich in 1870–1 as: 'Extirpation of the German spirit in favour of the German Reich'. Since then the throat of the German spirit has been well and truly cut. When in the last five or six years three-quarters of the world fell upon what was once Germany—I am not concerned now with apportioning blame, with the rights and wrongs of the situation—all that was really left for them to attack was the corpse of German cultural life. This does not mean, though, that it is now quite laid waste—no, German cultural life cannot be written off in spite of all the difficulties still to come. For what, ultimately, has led to the Germans' downfall? We must try to look at this honestly and openly. Their downfall was actually caused by the fact that they wanted to get involved in materialism without having any real talent for it. Others have a considerable talent in this direction. But the Germans, as Hermann Grimm put it so well, retreat when it would be better to advance, and rush in when they ought to exercise restraint.[11] Goethe is a good example of this. Although he had the capacity to formulate and develop a spirituality in works such as *Faust* or *Wilhelm Meister* which could have revolutionized the world, he couldn't take the final step that would have led him to the threshold of spiritual science. In his outer life, instead, this man of genius became a portly official of the Weimar court, who, though extremely industrious as a minister, ended up making all kinds of compromises, especially in political life.

We should recognize that the likes of Goethe and Humboldt represent possible beginnings, the untapped potential of German evolution that we should not ignore or dismiss if we wish to turn this evolution in a positive direction. For that great talent for abstraction, for elevating things to their most abstruse and rarefied state, is not one the Germans possess in any great measure; the further west we go, the more developed is this 'talent'. People think that German cultural life is rooted in abstractions only because they cannot experience its real nature: having squeezed the life out of their own culture, they imagine that that of others is also lifeless. The Germans really do not possess a gift for pressing forward to ultimate heights of abstraction. This is clear above all in the very unfortunate and miserable way their state and government is organized. If they had always had an innate talent for monarchy, as the French have to this day, they would never have fallen prey to 'Wilhelmism'. There would have been no need for them to choose or keep in office so strange a caricature of a monarch. The French may call themselves republicans, yet they still have in their midst an invisible monarch who holds the state and its structure together and keeps a stranglehold on people's hearts and minds—the spirit of Louis XIV, still omnipresent. This spirit, though now in a decadent form, still holds sway.

A still greater talent for abstraction, the greatest of all in the realm of external, political life, is expressed in the person of Woodrow Wilson. Those fourteen points of his, dispensed by this 'world-schoolmaster' to his wayward pupils, are all stamped with impracticality and unfeasability. They could come only from the spirit of abstraction itself that has no sense for true realities. There are perhaps two things that cultural-historical studies of the future will find hard to fathom. One is the Kant-Laplace theory of a universal fog-soup out of which all Creation is supposed to have distilled and crystallized. Hermann Grimm again found a very telling way of putting it, saying that the sight of a hungry dog circling a stinking bone is more appetising than such fantasies about cosmic evolution.

The other is the unbelievable fact that such large numbers of people could ever have taken the humbug of Woodrow

Wilson's fourteen points so seriously, in an age confronted by such real and dire social problems.

When we look at the way things in the world relate to one another, we discover that the economic life, the political life of rights, and the cultural life are all intertwined and entangled. If we want to avoid being pulled under by a cultural life and rights life that are degenerate in the extreme, we have no choice but to organize society in a threefold way. In such a society the economic life will grow out of independent roots. It wants to flourish and grow but cannot do so unless the cultural and rights spheres come towards it in freedom. People today must learn to see how the economic life, working its way into the social fabric via Anglo-American attitudes and thought-patterns, is just creeping along close to the ground; and that it will only be able to climb upwards if it works in harmony with what goes on in the whole of the rest of the world, in all other spheres, works to support the quite different aspects and talents of those not involved in its own sphere of activity. If this does not happen, we will be faced with the catastrophic possibility of a world wholely dominated by economic factors.

At the other end of the scale, if the world continues under the cultural influence of the declining, degenerating stream of ancient eastern wisdom, what was once highest truth and revelation will rush headlong into the most terrible deceit and falsehood. Nietzsche described how even the Greeks had to defend themselves against such untruth by means of their art.[12] Art is in the end the divine child who preserves us from sinking into falsehood, who redresses the balance of this cultural stream which otherwise ends in lies and error. Lies and deceit have become more widespread among civilized humanity in the last five or six years than in the whole of the preceding history of the world. Hardly a single public statement or pronouncement has had the stamp of truth.

So this stream bears us headlong into lies (see drawing page 156); and the middle one here draws us into selfishness and self-obsession. And if the Anglo-American-style economic life which threatens to dominate the world does not allow itself to be permeated by an independent cultural and spiritual life, and an independent life of rights and government, it will carry us on into a third abyss. There are three types of degeneracy which humanity is in danger of: the first under Ahriman's influence is the abyss of falsehood; the second under the sway of Lucifer is selfishness and self-seeking; the third abyss expresses itself in the physical realm as sickness and death and in the cultural realm as the sickness and death of culture.

The Anglo-American world may well achieve world-dominion; and without a threefold ordering of human society this dominion will spread cultural sickness and death through every region of the globe. Such a poisoned chalice is the gift of the Asuras,[13] in the same way that falsehood is Ahriman's gift and selfishness that of Lucifer.

The clarity we gain about these things should fire us with enthusiasm for seeking ways to enlighten as many people as possible. This is the urgent task for those who have some understanding, some insight into the realities at work. We must do all in our power to counter the dumb, blind mutton that thinks itself the lamb of wisdom, thinks it has achieved such marvels, with what we can gain from anthroposophy, from a practical implementation of the science of the spirit.

If these words have succeeded in rousing in you some sense of the deep seriousness inherent in these things, then I have perhaps achieved a little of what I intended. When we meet again in a few weeks' time, we shall continue to examine this theme. My intention today was to awaken in you a sense that our most important social efforts in these times must be to spread understanding of these things to as many people as possible.

V. '666' AND THE FUTURE OF HUMANITY—THE TASK OF MANICHAEISM

1. How Do I Find the Christ?

Last week we were speaking about the human soul's participation in the world of spirit, about how this must be our endeavour as we move on into the future.[1] I would now like to take this further by examining various things connected with the kind of experience of the Christ Mystery for which such ideals as I recently described, spiritual ideals, should prepare the way.

I beg you, firstly, simply to take as a statement of fact, though I will try to elaborate and clarify it in the course of this lecture, that the science of the spirit finds in the human soul's relationship to the body on the one hand, and the spirit on the other, a threefold relationship and inclination to the world of spirit.

Those who have no desire whatever to acquaint themselves with this world of spirit must undermine and deny this threefold inclination. But it is nevertheless present in all of us, as an urge firstly to perceive the divine in general, then—we are speaking, of course, of human beings at our present evolutionary stage—to perceive the Christ, and thirdly to perceive what is usually called the spirit or the Holy Spirit.

You are, of course, aware that there are people who deny all three. During the course of the nineteenth century in particular, when things at least in Europe were taken to extremes, we have had ample opportunity to experience this wholesale rejection of the divine.

The science of the spirit, which cannot doubt the existence of divine, supersensible worlds, can ask why it is that people have come to deny the whole divine realm—the *Father* of the Trinity. It can show us that wherever people deny the Father—that is, the whole divine nature indwelling the world, the divine which is recognized, to give just one example, in the Hebrew religion—then a real physical defect, a physical ailment or disability, occurs in the human body. The scientist of the spirit regards atheism as a form of illness, though of course it is one which doctors cannot cure—they themselves are often afflicted by it. It is not one recognized as such by contemporary medicine. The science of the spirit diagnoses this illness wherever people deny or reject what their body, not their soul, must in the healthy and natural course of things impart to them—that the world is interwoven with the divine.

There is a further kind of denial to which many are prone, a denial of Christ. The science of the spirit must regard this as a matter of destiny, connected with the human soul. It is forced to consider it a kind of misfortune. To deny God is an illness, to deny Christ a misfortune. Whether people find their way to Christ or not is really a matter of personal destiny, something influenced by individual karma.

To deny the spirit or the Holy Spirit, finally, points to a dullness of one's own spirit. We consist of body, soul and spirit. All three can suffer from a defect or disability. Atheism is an ailment that affects the physical body. Not to find our way to a connection with the world which Christ reveals to us is a misfortune. Not to find access to the spirit dwelling within us is a kind of dullness, a refined sort of idiocy, though not one usually recognized or understood.

But then we must ask how people can find their way to Christ. And that is the particular theme I would like to address today—how in the course of life the human soul can find its way to the Christ. This very question is often voiced by people who are genuinely and earnestly seeking an answer. But we cannot really get to grips with it without being aware of its broader historical context.

From a spiritual-scientific point of view, our present historical period began in the fifteenth century, in about the year 1413 in fact. The human soul at that time acquired the nature and constitution that it still has nowadays. Modern historical research does not perceive this, sees only outer facts. Its convenient fictions have no inkling of the fact that before the fifteenth century people thought, felt, acted in a different way, that their souls were quite differently constituted. The epoch that came to an end in 1413 had begun around 747BC, in the eighth century BC. This is why the science of the spirit dates what it calls the Graeco-Latin cultural epoch from 747BC to AD1413. Roughly at the end of the first third of this epoch occurred the Mystery of Golgotha.

For centuries this Mystery of Golgotha was the focal point of many people's feeling and thinking. In the times immediately preceding the advent of the new epoch that dawned in the fifteenth and sixteenth centuries, the human soul grasped this Event very strongly in the realm of feeling. Then, at the dawn of our modern times, the Gospels began to be read among broad sections of the populace. And soon disputes and disagreements started about whether they derived from true historical tradition. This sort of debate and argument has continued on into our own day, becoming more and more extreme. I don't wish to examine the detailed process and phases of this debate about the Mystery of Golgotha, which was of particular importance in Protestant theological circles, but to draw your attention to what people were aiming to achieve by means of it.

In this materialistic age people have got used to expecting material proofs for everything. Historical research only regards as 'proven' anything that is substantiated by documents and records. If there are written records of an historical event people assume that it really occurred. It is not really possible to attribute this sort of certainty to the Gospels. As I wrote in my book *Christianity as Mystical Fact*,[2] the Gospels are not historical documents at all but books of inspiration and inititation. In fact, none of the records of which the Bible is composed are truly historical. An unjustifiably highly-regarded theologian, *Adolf Harnack*,[3] has stated that all the genuine historical knowledge we have about Jesus Christ could be written on the back of a postcard. He is wrong in this only to the extent that even a postcard's-worth of substantiated evidence is not available. None of it is based on genuine, contemporary documentation! There are no accounts or records of the Mystery of Golgotha which could stand up to historical scrutiny. It is therefore impossible to 'prove' it by external means.

But there is a good reason for this. It *ought* not to be verifiable by external means, but only through the inspirations of divine wisdom: this most important Event of all earthly evolution should only be perceptible to supersensible vision, not provable in outer, materialistic terms. Those who wish to provide outer evidence of it will find that they cannot, that there is, in fact, none to be found. Humanity must come to realize that precisely the Mystery of Golgotha demands something different from them: that either they must seek to understand it by supersensible means or not at all. It should force the human soul to dispense with material proof and search for a path into the supersensible realm. This, then, is the whole import and significance of the science of the spirit. All outer science and research based on material proof will fail to provide any real knowledge of the Mystery of Golgotha; even theology will appear in a critical, unchristian guise. The science of the spirit will therefore take up the task of leading humanity to a true recognition of the Mystery of Golgotha on the path I have often described, which develops supersensible knowledge.[4]

Now let us look at the condition in which humanity found itself at the time of the Mystery of Golgotha, in the fourth post-Atlantean cultural epoch, the Graeco-Latin. Humanity evolves, one can say, by passing through the various levels and conditions of which we are composed. In the preceding Egyptian-Chaldean period, which ended around 747BC, humanity passed through the stage of the sentient soul. In the Graeco-Latin period it evolved through the stage of the mind soul;* and since the year 1413, the beginning of the fifth post-Atlantean epoch, it has been developing the consciousness soul. We can therefore say that at the period we are considering—the fourth, Graeco-Latin epoch—humanity was being educated to make free use of the mind soul.

Now let us enquire what the date of the midpoint of this epoch would have been, for there would of course have been a midpoint between 747BC and AD1413, up to which the mind soul was waxing; then waning, declining thereafter. You can easily work this out yourselves—this midpoint fell in the year 333 after the birth of Jesus Christ. This is a very important date, an important point in humanity's evolution, the midpoint of the Graeco-Latin epoch, 333 years after Jesus Christ's birth—after what then led to the Mystery of Golgotha.

We can only truly evaluate the condition of humanity in this epoch if we ask ourselves what would have happened if the Mystery of Golgotha had not happened. Humanity would then have had only its own elemental forces to carry it through to the year 333, to the midpoint of the epoch. It would still, from its own innate powers, have developed the capacities inherent in the mind soul, and would have continued to possess these in the coming centuries.

But this natural, innate process was directly and essentially altered by the Mystery of Golgotha. Something enormously and wholely different occurred. If we wish to characterize this unique Event which gave the whole earth a sense and purpose, we must regard the fact that only supersensible perception can give us access to this Mystery as the most important thing of all.

Why? Because although the human being of the fourth post-Atlantean epoch was by the year 333 approaching the

* In the original German, Steiner uses the *two* terms: Verstandesseele *and* Gemütsseele. The first means 'rational' or mind soul; the second means, roughly, 'heart-and-mind soul'. The German word 'Gemüt' has connotations of the 'thinking heart'.

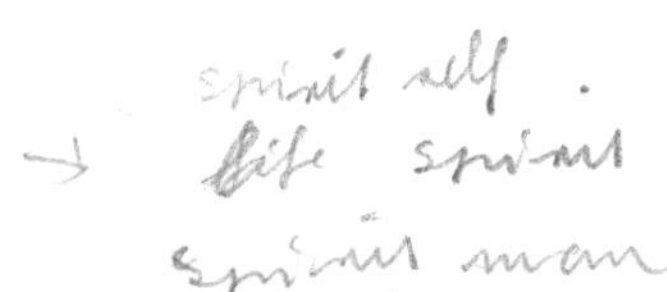

fullest flowering and culmination of the mind soul, he was still nowhere near understanding the nature of the Mystery of Golgotha by means of his normal, innate powers between birth and death. You see, although our own innate, bodily forces can allow us to develop through a lifetime and become old and ancient, they cannot enable us to grasp the Mystery of Golgotha.

The contemporaries of Christ Jesus, the disciples, the apostles who loved and surrounded him, could only understand and perceive Christ by means of atavistic clairvoyance. But this was not available to them through their own innate, human forces. And the Gospel writers wrote down the Gospels only by drawing on ancient Mystery books. These mighty Gospels were not written by virtue of the natural, innate forces which human beings had evolved up to that point, but through ancient, atavistic, clairvoyant powers.

But the human soul continues to evolve after it has passed over the threshold of death. This evolving human soul increases in understanding after death, learns to recognize and understand more and more.

Now what is remarkable is that the contemporaries of Christ whose love for Christ had prepared them for a life in Christ after death, only grasped the full import of the Mystery of Golgotha through their own innate human powers in the third century AD. Those, in other words, who had lived with Christ on earth as His apostles and disciples, died and lived on in the spiritual world, and as they did so their powers and forces increased, just as they do here on earth. We have less understanding at our death than we do 200 years later—we continue to evolve. Not until the second or third century AD did the contemporaries of Christ dwelling in the spiritual realms between death and rebirth reach the point of full understanding, through their own powers, of what they had experienced on the earth 200 or 300 years before. And then, from the spiritual worlds, they inspired the people who were below on the earth.

If you adopt this point of view and then read what the Church fathers received as inspiration and wrote down in the second and third centuries AD, you will be able to see how what they wrote can be understood. The inspiration they received from the contemporaries of Christ in the spiritual world is expressed in a remarkable kind of language, one which is almost wholely incomprehensible to people nowadays.

Let me cite one example—though I could perfectly well take someone else—of a person considered by our modern culture as quite unworthy of regard, for he coined a quite dreadful phrase: *Credo quia absurdum est*—'I believe what is absurd and not what is reasonable'. This was Tertullian.[5]

One can gain a quite particular impression from reading this Tertullian, who lived roughly at the time that inspiration from the dead contemporaries of Christ started to flow down, and who reflected this inspiration as well as a human being may who is endowed with a particular constitution and temperament. One can only express inspiration in the form in which one receives it, which is always affected by one's own constitution. Tertullian could therefore not give pure expression to this inspiration, but communicated it only in the way which his human brain was capable of, and in the form his particular rather passionate and fanatical character dictated. He just wrote everything down as it came to him—and we can see that it came to him in an extremely curious form if we examine it from a true perspective.

Such a perspective shows Tertullian to have been a Roman who lacked a high level of literary finesse and education, yet was still capable of pouring a wonderful power into his written language. He is, one can say, the first person to have adapted Latin to express Christianity. He managed to infuse this most prosaic and unpoetic of languages, this language of dry rhetoric, with such temperament and holy passion that in his hands it really expresses the fresh immediacy of the soul—particularly in *De Carne Christi*, for example, or in the volume in which he tries to dismiss all the accusations levelled at the Christians. These works are written with a holy fervour and with wonderful intensity of language. He did not allow his own Roman-ness to prejudice his views, but magnificently defended the Christians against Roman persecution, attacking the way they were so mistreated in attempts to make them deny their adherence to Christ Jesus. 'Surely,' he said, 'there is ample proof of your unjust judging of the Christians. You should turn to quite different methods when you call the Christians to account, for usually you apply such mistreatment in order to get at the truth—not, as you do with the Christians, to force people to deny what they believe by torturing them. Against the Christians you are proceeding in a quite opposite way from your usual approach: the normal aim of your justice is to expose the truth; but your aim with the Christians is to compel them to avow deceit and falsehood.' So Tertullian took his stand, with such arguments which hit the nail on the head.

As well as being a brave and powerful man who saw through the empty rituals of Roman worship and voiced what he saw, he was also someone whose words showed a real connection with the world of spirit. He spoke about this world in a way that shows he knew what he was talking about. He spoke of demons as familiarly as of other human beings. 'Just ask a demon,' he said, 'whether the Christ of the Christians is a true god!' He knew, you see, that demons do not lie. They hate and struggle against Christ because He *is* divine. 'Confront a possessed person, inhabited by a demon, with a true Christian: if you manage to make the demon speak, he will tell you the truth, will reveal his real, demonic nature in the face of Christ.' Tertullian called upon demons as well as human beings to bear witness to the truth—these were ideas that came from him, not from any received tradition.

So what, one is fully justified in asking, was Tertullian's deeper, soul-grounded, inspired belief? He actually had inklings of something that would not really dawn on humanity until long after his own time. His belief could basically be formulated in three principles about human nature: first, that at that time, the end of the second century AD, the human being had the shameful capacity to deny the greatest event of all earth evolution; and that to follow his own innate tendencies would not lead him to any knowledge or understanding of this event. Secondly, that the human soul was too weak to grasp this greatest earthly occurrence. And thirdly, that it was quite impossible for anyone to find a real connection with the Mystery of Golgotha by following only the dictates and capacities of his mortal, human body.

These three things roughly sum up Tertullian's belief. On the basis of them he formulated the following passage:

'God's Son was crucified: because this is disgraceful it is no disgrace. He died: because this is absurd it is believable.'[6] ('Prorsus credibile est, quia ineptum est'. This is the actual phrase to be found in Tertullian, not the one the world holds against him—'Credo, quia absurdum est, I believe what is absurd'—which does not occur either in his works or in those of any other Church father.) And thirdly, says Tertullian: 'He who was buried has risen, because it is impossible. We must believe it because it is impossible.'

Tertullian's threefold saying quoted here naturally appears appalling to modern, sharp-witted minds. Just imagine a modern, squeaky-clean materialist's reaction to such words: 'Christ was crucified; we must believe it because it is shameful. Christ died; we must believe it because it is absurd. Christ truly rose again; we must believe it because it is impossible.' A dyed-in-the-wool monist wouldn't be able to make head or tail of such words!

So what did Tertullian mean? The inspiration he received helped him to gain a true understanding of the human beings of his time, of the state and stage at which human nature had then arrived, at the midpoint of the fourth post-Atlantean epoch. In as many years more, 333, as had already passed since the Mystery of Golgotha—which would take us to the year 666—certain spiritual powers had intended to lead earthly evolution in quite different directions from the evolutionary path it actually followed as a result of the Mystery of Golgotha. AD666 is the date of which the author of the Apocalypse spoke with such vehemence.[7] Just read for yourselves the relevant passage, in which the writer of the Apocalypse describes all that 666 signifies! The intention of certain spiritual forces would have been fulfilled if the Mystery of Golgotha had not intervened. From the year 333 onwards, the point of culmination and flowering of the mind soul, a downward path would have drawn humanity into quite different regions than had been foreseen by those divine beings connected with us from the very beginning, from the Saturn phase. This would have happened by means of a kind of premature revelation to humanity, by the year 666 already, of the nature and content of the consciousness soul. If this had happened then the aim of certain beings opposed to human evolution, who desired to appropriate this evolution for themselves, would have been achieved. The human being would have been overwhelmed, in 666, by a quality of consciousness soul that it will now not attain for a long time still to come.

This is the course invariably adopted by those beings hostile to the gods who love the human being: they try to force premature development upon a humanity not yet mature enough to deal with it. The luciferic and ahrimanic forces aimed to inject the human being in the year 666 with the capacity to grasp his own individuality in full consciousness—an evolutionary step that really belongs to the middle of our own present epoch, one which should take place 1080 years after 1413, in the year 2493.

If these beings had succeeded in their adversarial aims, if they had managed to graft the consciousness soul on to the human being, they would have made it impossible for him to pursue his further path towards the spirit-self, the life-spirit and the spirit-man. The human being's path to the future would have been blocked off, and he would have been diverted in a quite different evolutionary direction.

Yet although things did not get diverted and side-tracked in this phenomenal, grandiose yet diabolic way, the traces of such influence can still be found in the course history took. Certain things occurred which are symptomatic of the influence of spiritual beings working through human beings on earth, using them as their instruments. The Emperor Justinian[8] was one such 'agent', an enemy of all that had survived of the higher wisdom of ancient Greece, who closed down the schools of philosophy in Athens in 529 so that the last vestiges of Greek knowledge, of Aristotelian-Platonic wisdom, were suppressed and forced over into Persia. It was here also, at Nisibis, that some time before, in the fifth century, the scholars and wise men of Syria had arrived after Zeno Isauricus[9] had driven them away from Odessa. Here, then, in the Persian *Academy of Gondishapur*, not long before the year 666, was gathered together the best of all that remained of ancient Greek wisdom, which had taken no notice or account of the Mystery of Golgotha. And within this academy scholars taught who were inspired by luciferic-ahrimanic forces.

If the intentions of these spiritual powers had been fulfilled, and the year 666 had brought upon humanity a premature injection with the consciousness soul which would have short-circuited its future evolution, if, in other words, the intentions of the Gondishapur academy had been fulfilled, then in the seventh century there would have arisen many very scholarly, highly educated, extremely gifted geniuses who, wandering through West Asia, North Africa, Southern Europe, in fact through all of Europe, would have spread the '666' culture far and wide. This culture would have been one, above all, which rooted the human being in his own individuality, which focused the qualities of the consciousness soul with great intensity.

This did not and could not come about. The world had become a different place. The whole impetus and influence which would have radiated out from the Gondishapur academy into the culture of the West was dulled and diverted. Instead of a wisdom compared with which all our present external knowledge would be insignificant—instead of a mighty, glorious wisdom simply channelled into people by spiritual means about everything that we have had to slowly and gradually work towards in outer experimental science, and will continue to work towards up to the year 2493—only vestiges remained, traces which found their way into what Arab scholars brought over to Spain. The whole impetus was blunted, and all that remained was Mohammedanism, the teachings of *Mohammed.*[10] The teachings of Islam were all that remained of the influence of the Gondishapur academy. The Mystery of Golgotha redressed the balance and brought the world back from the edge of a tendency that would have spelt its ruin.

And the world's redemption became possible not only because the Mystery of Golgotha took place, but also because it occurred in a way that cannot be understood through the forces normally available to us during life; and by means of which the circumstances I described to you came about—of inspiration flowing towards people within western culture from those who had died, as we can find in Tertullian and many others of that time. As a result, people's attention was drawn to the Mystery of Golgotha—in a quite different direction, therefore, from the exalted, yet diabolic wisdom that was intended to emanate from the Gondishapur Academy. Although this inspiration from the dead came through in partial and fragmentary ways, it was able to hinder the spread of diabolic wisdom and serve the greater good of humanity, protect humanity from the impulses it would otherwise have been defenceless against.

But such impulses carry on invisibly, behind the corridors of outer evolution. Such things have a definite effect in supersensible realms; we cannot judge either the intentions of the Gondishapur Academy or the Event of Golgotha according to their manifestations on the physical plane. If we are really to describe such things with any accuracy, we have to seek their ramifications in far more profound depths than we usually plumb.

Humanity has been subject to a residual influence from all that was intended, that was then obstructed and hindered so that instead of something magnificent and overwhelming, we were left with the pitiful fantasies of Islam.* The residual effect upon a humanity exposed to the Gondishapur impulse, the neo-Persian impulse that brought with it an inappropriate resurgence of the Zarathustra impulse,[11] was, if I may put it crudely, an inner crack or fault spreading right into our physical constitution. Ever since, we continue to be born with this defect—the kind of sickness that I spoke of earlier, a tendency to deny God the Father.

Let's be clear about this: civilized humanity has a thorn in its side. St Paul speaks of this thorn a good deal,[12] and what he says is prophetic: he was a particularly advanced individual—most people didn't begin to feel the thorn until the seventh century. This thorn will lodge itself deeper and deeper in us, will influence us more and more. People who are strongly affected by this thorn nowadays—who suffer from this ailment, for that is what it is—become atheists, deny the divine. Every single person belonging to modern, western civilization has a predisposition to atheism; whether he gives himself up to it or not is another matter. We all carry within us the germs of a sickness that in a fully-blown state will lead us to reject the divine, although our innate disposition is really to affirm it. Our nature has become somewhat mineralised, our evolu-

---

* Publisher's note: In his lecture of 16 October 1918, Rudolf Steiner balances this statement by pointing to 'the wisdom in world-history' that introduced Islam 'to deaden the Gnostic wisdom of Gondishapur, to take from it the strong ahrimanically seductive force which would otherwise have been exercised upon mankind.' (*Three Streams in Human Evolution*, Rudolf Steiner Press, London 1965, p.89.)

tionary stature has shrunk under the wasting effect of this God-denying ailment.

This sickness has brought about a stronger force of attraction between the human soul and body than was previously the case, and than our innate human nature would otherwise give rise to. The soul has as it were been welded on to the body. It is not the soul's innate nature to share in the fate of the body; but this would increasingly have been the case—the soul would have been compelled to immerse itself in the physical destiny of birth, heredity and death.

The wisdom of the Gondishapur Academy had a quite specific aim and intention, one which certain secret societies of our own time also share, though in a more dilettantish form—nothing less than an enormous advancement of humanity's earthly powers that would go hand in hand with subjection to the forces of death, so that people passing through the gates of death would lose all inclination to imbue themselves with spirit and to take part in successive incarnations. The aim was to cut short the further evolution of the human being, and instead to appropriate his powers for a quite different realm—to preserve and incarcerate him in a wholely earthly perspective, so that he would lose all sight of the long, slow, gradual process of evolution towards the spirit-self, the life-spirit and the spirit-man.

The human soul would therefore have become more profoundly acquainted with the earth than destiny had intended. Death, that should only affect the body, would have come to be the soul's fate as well. The Mystery of Golgotha worked against this: the human being became acquainted with death, it is true, but at the same time was protected from complete immersion in death by the Mystery of Golgotha. To balance the stronger connection which had come about between soul and body, Christ bound the soul more strongly to the spirit than had been intended. Through the Mystery of Golgotha, the human soul came closer to the spirit than had been predestined.

This can open up for us a long perspective, so that we see the intimate connection between the Mystery of Golgotha and the inner forces at work in human nature through the millennia. To gain a true idea of the place of the Mystery of Golgotha in human history and evolution, one must be able to compare the interrelationship between body and soul, subject to the sway of Lucifer and Ahriman, with the interrelationship between the soul and spirit.

The Catholic Church, which was strongly [influenced] by vestiges of the impulses emanating from the Gondishapur Academy, made the dogmatic decree in 869, at the Eighth Ecumenical Council,[13] that people should not believe in the spirit. Its aim was actually to spread a veil of darkness over the Mystery of Golgotha, not to enlighten all mankind. The Catholic Church abolished the spirit in 869. The dogma it instated at that time implies that there is no such thing as spirit, only body and soul. True, it conceded that the soul has 'something' of a spiritual quality, but nevertheless rejected the threefold, body-soul-spirit constitution of the human being. This act of abolition was directly influenced by the Gondishapur impulse. But history does not obey the dictates or manipulations of human beings.

The human being's connection with the spirit was in fact strengthened by the Mystery of Golgotha, so that two diverging tendencies balanced each other out: the force which acquaints our soul with death, and the one which frees us from death again, which leads us inwardly to the spirit.

What is this force? I have said that denial of the divine is a kind of sickness. The predisposition for this denial is a sort of affliction which all civilized human beings carry within them, within their physical body. We can't do anything about this predisposition, it's just there inside us, but we can progress beyond it, can cease denying the divine by finding God once more through Christ. Against the God-denying force, the affliction in our bodies, we can, since the Mystery of Golgotha, set the Christ-force, a health-bringing, healing power within us. Christ is truly the Saviour, the healer, the doctor who can cure the sickness of God-denial. He can cure this condition I have been speaking of.

Our time is seeing in very many respects a resurgence of currents which originated with the Mystery of Golgotha on one hand, and with the year 333, and the year 666, on the other. This has quite specific results. You can only properly understand the Mystery of Golgotha if you are clear that it *cannot* be understood through the unaided forces we are endowed with in physical life between birth and death. Even Christ's contemporaries, the contemporaries of the disciples and apostles, could only gradually come to an understanding of it out of their own human powers—not until the third century, in fact, long after their death. But all these things implant themselves and have an effect on evolution. One such effect is the following:

Today we are in a quite different position from the contemporaries of Christ, or those who lived up until the seventh century. We are now, in the twentieth century, well into the fifth post-Atlantean epoch. That means that we bring with us into birth, when we descend from supersensible into sense realms, experiences we have had centuries before in the spiritual world. The contemporaries of Christ, of the Mystery of Golgotha, only gained understanding of this Mystery several centuries afterwards; and we experience a kind of mirror-image, a reflection of it, hundreds of years before we come to birth. This is only true of people who are born today, it is something new. People being born today bring with them into the physical world a 'cloud of glory' from the Mystery of Golgotha, a reflection of what they have experienced in the spiritual world centuries after that Event.

Those who do not have supersensible perception cannot of course have direct vision of this impulse, but they can experience its effect within themselves. And when they experience it they discover an answer to the question: How do I find the Christ?

For this to happen, the following experiences are needed. First, of undertaking to strive for self-knowledge to the extent allowed by one's very individual, personal human capacities. Everyone who is honest in this striving will have to concede that he cannot actually attain what he seeks, that his powers are insufficient, that he feels weak and powerless to achieve his aims. This is a very important experience, one which every person must have who genuinely seeks self-knowledge. The feeling of incapacity and powerlessness is healthy, for it is nothing other than a sense of the illness and ailment afflicting us, which is the first step on the path to recovery—for those who suffer from an illness and do not even know they are ill are in the worst state of all. The feeling that we are powerless to elevate ourselves to the divine is an expression of this illness I spoke of that has been implanted in us. Experiencing this illness within ourselves gives us a sense of the soul as burdened by the body's mortality—that it too would have to die. If we experience this feeling of powerlessness strongly enough then we can suddenly turn the corner, receive the opposite experience: the feeling that if we refrain from immersing ourselves in what our physical powers alone can provide, if we immerse ourselves instead in the gifts of the spirit, then we can overcome this inner soul-death. We can find our soul again and unite with the spirit. We can sense the emptiness of existence on one hand and its glorification through ourselves on the other, once we step beyond our feelings of powerlessness. We can sense our illness and incapacity through our powerlessness; but we can also sense the Saviour, the healing power, by plumbing the depths of this powerlessness and acquainting our souls with death. When we sense the Healer we feel that we bear something in our soul that can at any moment resurrect from death within our own inner experience. These two experiences belong together. When we seek both of them we can find Christ within our own soul.

This is an experience which humanity is progressing towards. *Angelus Silesius* expressed it in these significant words:

The Cross of Golgotha cannot set us free
From evil, if not raised in you and me.[14]

We can raise it in ourselves by sensing the two poles of powerlessness through our body, and resurrection through our spirit.

The inner experience thus gained leads us surely towards the Mystery of Golgotha. Having supersensible powers of perception is not necessary for grasping this Event, and not having them is no reason to ignore it. All that anyone needs is to exercise real self-knowledge and have the will to combat the ubiquitous pride that conceals from people the fact that their own strength and capacity is not the be-all and end-all. If we cannot penetrate the veil of our own pride to recognize that our own unaided capacities leave us powerless, then we can experience neither death nor resurrection, can never really understand Angelus Silesius' words:

The Cross of Golgotha cannot set us free
From evil, if not raised in you and me.

But when we plumb the depths of powerlessness and then experience renewal, we can be graced with a real relationship to Christ Jesus. For this experience is a recapitulation of something we have experienced hundreds of years before in the spiritual world. So we must seek its reflection in our soul here on earth. Look within and you will find powerlessness. Seek further, go through the powerlessness, and you will find redemption from powerlessness, the resurrection of the soul into the spirit.

But don't allow yourselves to be led astray in your search by various mystical or even apparently positive confessions and faiths. When Harnack[15] speaks of Christ, for instance, his statements are not actually true, for what he attributes to

Christ applies to God and the divine in general. It applies just as well to the God of the Jews, the God of the Mohammedans, to all gods in general. And many today who desire to 'awake', who say that they experience the god within, are only in fact experiencing God the Father—and only in a diluted form—for they do not notice their affliction, and that they are only speaking in traditional, received forms. *Johannes Müller*[16] is such a one. None of these people have Christ, for Christ is not simply experienced in the human soul, but in two aspects: the death brought about in the soul through the physical body, and resurrection of the soul through the spirit. Whoever in contrast—and unlike the merely rhetorical theosophists—can speak of powerlessness and resurrection from powerlessness, is speaking of a real Christ experience. Such a person finds himself upon a supersensible path towards the Mystery of Golgotha, finds in himself the forces which stimulate the development of certain supersensible capacities, and which lead him to the Mystery of Golgotha.

There is really no need nowadays to give up hope of finding one's way to direct, personal experience of Christ. Once one has passed through powerlessness and refinds oneself, one also finds Christ. Before we can gain access to the Christ Impulse we must plumb the depths of our own feelings of insignificance, and this can only happen when we view our own strength and capacities without any pride. Many mystics believe that finding the higher or divine ego within the personal ego is the same as Christianity, but it is not. Christianity stands on the foundation which these words express:

The Cross of Golgotha cannot set us free
From evil, if not raised in you and me.

We can feel the truth of this in the tiniest details of life; and from these specific, small details we can rise into an experience of powerlessness and resurrection from powerlessness. My dear friends, it would be good if people, particularly those of our circle, found their way to the following understanding:

There is, certainly, a desire for truth rooted in the depths of people's souls, a desire also to speak the truth. But precisely when we desire to express the truth and then become aware of this desire in ourselves, we can take a first step down the road of feeling the physical body's impotence and powerlessness in relation to divine truth. At the very moment that you become really aware of your own truth-speaking, you encounter something remarkable. A poet sensed something of this when he wrote: 'When the soul *speaks,* alas the *soul* no longer speaks.'[17] What we experience in our souls as truth grows dull, loses its edge on its way to become speech. It does not die altogether but it loses its force. Whoever understands language knows that the true designation for a thing is the proper noun which applies to it alone and nothing else. The moment we generalize—whether through nouns, verbs or adjectives—we begin to depart from the truth. Truth then consists in our awareness that every sentence we speak must be at variance with the truth. The science of the spirit tries to find ways to resurrect from this recognition of the untruth of everything one says. I have often mentioned that the *way* one says something is more important than *what* one says, for the latter succumbs to our incapacity and powerlessness. In my writings you will see that I have tried always to describe something from all sorts of different points of view. This is the only way to approach the truth of things. Anyone is mistaken who thinks words themselves are any more than a kind of eurythmy. Words are just eurythmic movements arising from the larynx and accompanied by the air. They are just gestures, not made by hands and body but by the larynx. We must become aware that our words only point to something, and that we only gain a right relationship to the truth when we see words as indicators or signposts pointing towards what we want to express; also when we live together in human communities in a way that shows awareness that signs and indications are alive in the words we speak. This is partly the aim of Eurythmy, which makes the whole human being into a larynx,[18] which expresses through the medium of the whole human being what is otherwise expressed only through the larynx, so that people begin once more to have a sense for the fact that the words they speak are only a kind of gesture. Such words as 'Father' or 'Mother' are concrete and specific. But when I speak in more general, abstract terms, I can only express myself truly by virtue of the fact that the other person I am speaking with has immersed himself together with me in the social context of the things we speak of, and is able to understand the gestures I make. We can only arise out of the ashes of powerlessness which we can sense even in language when we understand that we need to be Christian in the least expression that falls from our lips. What the Word, the Logos, has become in the course of evolution can only be understood when it is united once more with the Christ, when we become aware that our body, as tool of expression and language, forces truth downwards, suffocates it to some degree as it emerges on our lips. And we can revive truth, through Christ, when we become aware that we need to spiritualize it, which means looking beyond the forms of language and seeking the spirit, thinking our way through to the spirit. That, my dear friends, is something we need to learn.

I'm not yet sure if there will be enough time tomorrow to speak about such things in public.[19] I would like to, but let me at least say it here. If I should repeat myself tomorrow, please forgive me—I have already said this before, in public lectures. One can, you see, make a very interesting discovery, which I will illustrate with a particular instance: I have made a careful study of the really very interesting essays of Woodrow Wilson,[20] lectures about American history, American literature, American life. It is true to say that he has drawn a mighty and impressive picture of American development as it has spread from the American East Coast to the Far West. He writes as an American through and through, and his essays, based on his lectures, are fascinating. 'Mere Literature' he calls them, and they give a good deal of insight into the American character, of which he is a very typical representative. Now what I have done is to compare various things in Woodrow Wilson's essays—and this is a quite objective process—with things that someone like Herman Grimm[21] expressed, who was a thoroughly typical nineteenth-century German and Central European, and whose manner of writing I find as agreeable as I find Woodrow Wilson's disagreeable. But that is only my personal predilection: I love the way Herman Grimm writes, while Woodrow Wilson's style is something quite alien and distasteful to me—but we can get beyond the personal reaction and see, quite objectively, that this typical American, Woodrow Wilson, writes magnificently about the development of the American people and way of life. But my comparison did not stop there: I set particular passages of Grimm and Wilson next to each other, in which they both address methods of historical research. There are sentences and passages which are almost perfectly interchangeable, which are nearly identical word for word. And I am not suggesting that one borrowed from the other, far from it! Instead, such a comparison can perfectly illustrate that when two people say the same thing, they are in fact saying something different. But let us look a little closer, for this is problematic: what is actually going on here, when Woodrow Wilson describes his Americans in a far more insightful and suggestive way than Herman Grimm ever managed in his approach to historical method? What is strange about the fact that Woodrow Wilson describes these things in sentences that seem almost to have been lifted wholesale from passages of Herman Grimm?

If we look closer we find the following. In every sentence and passage that Herman Grimm wrote we can sense the personal, individual effort, the struggle. Everything he writes about is expressed from the viewpoint of nineteenth-century culture, but imbued with the direct promptings of the consciousness soul. Woodrow Wilson, on the other hand, describes things magnificently, but as though he is possessed by subconscious influences. There is a quality of demonic possession in his writings. Something in his subconscious inspires what he writes. The grandeur and magnificence of his descriptions is that of a daemon speaking through his soul, though of course in the particular style of a twentieth-century American.

Humanity has developed some lazy habits: one such is apparent in the way people think that two pieces of writing with similar content derive from similar sources. We have to learn now, instead, that the content itself is not nearly so important as the person who expresses it. We have to develop a sense for the person behind the words, behind the outer gestures, a sense for the source the words emanate from. My dear friends, this is a very great Mystery of ordinary life, for there is really a very great difference between the ego-centred labour of expressing things by working for them through individual effort and striving, and simply 'receiving' them from some source outside oneself—whether from above, below, or sideways if you like. Writing inspired from a source beyond the writer's ego is actually more inviting and suggestive; things expressed through conscious and conscientious effort demand more work from the reader, who must reproduce the process and some of the labour which the writer went through. And the time is not far off when our emphasis will have to shift from the content, the mere words, to the person behind the words—not the outer, physical character and personality, but the whole human and spiritual context.

This is the sort of answer that must be given when people ask how they may find Christ. Christ cannot be reached through any weird and wonderful notions, through any convenient mysticism or hocus pocus. We can only find Christ by having the courage to get to grips with life. When you do this you will start to sense the impotence which the body, by becoming the instrument of language, has saddled you with; and also, then, the spirit's resurrection in the Word. That is the point. Not only 'The letter killeth, but the spirit giveth life', but even the spoken word killeth and the spirit must be resurrected once more by connecting each separate experience to the Christ and the Mystery of Golgotha in a real and specific way. Christ can be found by taking this first step: seeking, not just for insight into the content of fine-sounding words—which is the habit people have developed nowadays—but for the human context, for the source the words stem from. This will become more and more important. If some among us would give more thought to this, they would not come rushing up to say: 'Just read what this person has written—it sounds really anthroposophical!' The words in themselves are not what count, but the spirit underlying them. It is not words that we wish to spread through anthroposophy, but a new spirit, one which must be the spirit of Christianity from the twentieth century onwards.

That, my dear friends, is what I wished to add to the things I said a week ago. I am glad that I had the opportunity to speak to you again about these matters that concern us all closely, and I hope that we can continue these branch-meeting discussions here in Zurich in the very near future. But even when we are separated by distance, we can remember that as anthroposophists our souls are in close contact, and that we may if we so wish remain always close and true in spirit, the spirit of humanity that should hold sway in all that we do.

2. The Future of Human Evolution

We have repeatedly said that our seven cultural ages will end with the War of All against All;[1] now this war must really be imagined quite differently fom the way we have been accustomed to think of wars. We must bear in mind its source and real cause, which is the increase of human egotism, of self-seeking and selfishness. And we have now reached the point in our observations of seeing what a sharp two-edged sword the human ego is. Those who fail to grasp the double-edged nature of the ego will hardly be able to understand the whole sense and purpose of human and world evolution. From one point of view, the ego causes people to grow inwardly hard, to draw into the service of the ego all that may be available to them in the form either of outer things or inner capacities. The ego itself is what causes us to direct all our desires towards satisfying it. Its striving to appropriate for itself a part of what really belongs to all the earth, to drive all other egos away from its own realm, to fight them and be at war with them, is one side of the ego. But we must not forget that the ego also makes us independent, gives us our inner freedom, which in the truest sense of the word elevates and exalts us. Our worth and dignity is founded in this ego. It is our potential for the divine.

This concept of the ego presents difficulties for many people. We know, of course, that the human ego has developed out of a group-soul nature, from a kind of all-inclusive universal ego from which it separated itself out. It would be wrong to want to submerge our ego once more in some kind of universal and common consciousness. Only weakness causes people to long to lose their separate ego and dissolve into universal consciousness. Only those people really understand the nature of the ego who recognize that it can no longer be cast away once it has been acquired in the course of cosmic evolution. And if we understand the mission of the world aright, we know that we must strive to strengthen ourselves so that the ego becomes ever more inward and divine. True anthroposophists have no interest at all in the ego's dissolution and submersion in a universal self, in melting away into some sort of primeval gruel. True anthroposophy can only see its ultimate goal as the forming of a community of emancipated, independent and differentiated egos. This is the mission of the earth, expressed through love: that one ego learns to encounter another in freedom. No love is perfect that proceeds from coercion, from being linked or bound together through necessity. Only when each ego is so free and independent that it can choose *not* to love, is its love an entirely free gift. This is really the aim of the divine plan—to make the ego so independent that it can offer the free, individual gift of love even to God. If people remained even slightly compelled or coerced to love, they would still be attached to the apron strings of dependency.

The ego therefore represents the promise of the human being's highest goal. But if it does not find love, if it hardens inwardly, it is also the tempter that casts us into the abyss. Then it becomes what separates people from each other, leading them ultimately to the great War of All against All—not only the war of nation against nation (for the concept of nations will then no longer have anything like the significance it possesses today) but the war of each single individual against every other in all realms of life; the war of class against class, caste against caste, the war between different generations and races. In all realms of life, then, the ego will become the focus of strife and contention, which is why we can say that it can lead both to the highest and to the lowest possible qualities. So it is a sharp, two-edged sword. And the One who brought humanity the potential for full ego-consciousness, Christ Jesus, is as we have seen rightly symbolically portrayed in the Apocalypse with a sharp, two-edged sword in His mouth.

We have regarded as a great achievement the human being's ascent, specifically through Christianity, to this potential for free ego-hood. Christ Jesus brought this ego in its full compass and extent, which can only be expressed through this image of the sharp, two-edged sword familiar to you from our occult seals.[2] The fact that this sword proceeds from the mouth of the Son of Man is also comprehensible, for only once we had learnt to utter the 'I' in full consciousness was the power given us either to rise to the greatest heights or sink to the lowest depths. The sharp, two-edged sword is one of the most important symbols we encounter in the Apocalypse.

So if we clearly understand what was said at the close of the last lecture, that our present culture will be succeeded by what was described in church encyclicals as the Philadelphia community, then we will have to recognize that the human souls who are destined to pass over into following ages will be drawn from this Philadelphia stage, from the sixth cultural epoch. After the War of All against All, as I have often described, people's features will express all that in our age is being prepared in the human soul. The so-called seventh epoch will be of very little importance. We are now living in the fifth cultural epoch, which will be followed by the sixth, from which will proceed a number of people full of understanding for the world of spirit, imbued with the brotherly and sisterly love that arises through spiritual knowledge. The ripest fruit of our present culture will appear in the sixth cultural epoch. The following, seventh stage will bring lukewarm qualities, neither very hot nor cold, will manifest rather like an overripe fruit, as something which outlasts the War of All against All, but will not bear within itself any fertilizing principle of progress.

It was the same when our cultural epoch arose. Think of the time before the Atlantean flood: people then dwelt upon the terrain now covered by the Atlantic ocean, and in the last third of this epoch a community which had attained the highest stage of Atlantean civilization formed close to what is now

Ireland, and this group then migrated to the East, from where all later cultures proceeded. Keep this clearly in mind, think of this portion of the earth that is now covered by the ocean west of Ireland, imagine the migration of people from there towards the East; then tribes dispersing from there, spreading and populating Europe. The population of Europe formed in this way. The most highly developed Atlanteans migrated to central Asia, and from there evolved all the various cultures which finally led to our own, so that we can see that our present culture originated in a small group of Atlanteans.

Atlantis, however, had seven consecutive stages just as our own epoch has seven stages which we know as the ancient Indian, ancient Persian, Assyrian-Babylonian-Chaldean-Egyptian-Jewish, the Graeco-Latin, our own and two further ones.[3] It was in the fifth Atlantean stage that this migration began; so our own culture is founded on a specially chosen population from the fifth Atlantean race, for 'race' is an appropriate term in the context of Atlantis.[4] A sixth and a seventh followed, which were so to speak the 'luke-warm races'. They also survived the Flood, but there was no vital life and potential in them. They were related to the fifth Atlantean culture as the woody, hard outer bark is related to the living sap inside the stem. These two races which followed the real root-race had no potential within them for further evolution; they were 'overripe' one can say.

Still today you may see the last remnants and stragglers of these ancient, overripe races, especially in the Chinese people. One can see that their culture did not have any connection with what manifested in the fifth race, the root race, when the etheric body entered into the physical body so that human beings first began to develop the capacity to say 'I'. The Chinese people missed out this stage. This did, though, enable them to develop that high degree of culture and civilization which we are familiar with—but which was unable to evolve further. The fifth Atlantean race sent out the bearers of future culture, who created new civilizations with the capacity to grow and become ever more perfect. From ancient Indian times to our own culture everything has been growing and developing. But the sixth and seventh Atlantean races allowed themselves to become rigid and therefore static, and Chinese culture represents the last remnant of that. The ancient Chinese possessed a wonderful Atlantean heritage, but they could not advance beyond its zenith. One can trace these influences through careful observation: examine Chinese literature, which, though it has been subject to all sorts of other influences, nevertheless bears the mark of Atlantean character, expressed in a tendency to be inwardly self-contained, complete. This capacity for making inventions and discoveries yet taking them no further, being unable to advance to a new stage, is part and parcel of late-Atlantean nature.

Just as happened with the fifth Atlantean race, which provided certain groups of people with a vitality and capacity for further evolution, and with the sixth and seventh races which underwent a decline, so will it be in our own times. We are now striving forwards towards the sixth cultural epoch—to the stage that must be characterized as developing out of the spiritual marriage between West and East. The sixth cultural epoch will provide the foundation for the new cultures which will arise after the War of All against All, just as our cultures arose after the Atlantean epoch. The seventh cultural epoch, in contrast, will be one of decline, will be tepid. This seventh epoch will continue on into the new age, just as the sixth and seventh epochs of Atlantean times continued on into our own in the form of races which had become rigid and static. After the War of All against All, there will be two streams in humanity: on the one hand the cultural stream of Philadelphia will survive, containing the principle of progress, inner freedom and brotherly and sisterly love—a small band drawn from every tribe and nation; and on the other, the great mass of all those who will be tepid, the inheritors of those who are becoming tepid in our times, the stream of Laodicea. After the War of All against All, the evil stream will gradually be led over to good by the good race, the good cultural stream. This will be one of the chief tasks to be fulfilled after the great war: to rescue what can be rescued from those who will then be driven only to fight one another and express themselves in the most extreme egotism. Within occult spheres all such things are always allowed for in advance.

The fact that humanity will be divided into those who stand on the right and those who stand on the left should not be regarded as unduly severe, as something unjust and uncalled-for in the plan of Creation. Think of it rather as highest wisdom. Consider that through evil separating from good, the good will be immeasurably strengthened, and that after the great War of All against All the good will have to make every possible effort to salvage and rescue the evil, during the period in which this will still be possible. That will not be the kind of undertaking we think of as educative nowadays; occult forces will also be involved, for in this next great epoch people will understand how to set occult forces into motion. The good will have the task of working upon and affecting their kindred in the evil stream. This will all be prepared beforehand in occult world-streams, the deepest of which is least understood. The world-stream preparing these things says the following to its pupils: People speak of good and evil, but they do not know that it is necessary for evil, too, to increase and reach a peak, so that those who must overcome this evil can exercise their strength in overcoming it in such a way that a greater good results. The best of all humanity must be chosen and prepared for survival beyond the time of the great War of All against All, when people will oppose them who bear in their countenances the sign of evil; they must be so prepared that as many good forces as possible will flow into mankind. It will still be possible for those bodies which retain some degree of softness and flexibility to be transformed after the War of All against All by the souls of those who are open to conversion, who can still be guided towards the good in this last epoch. Much will thereby be gained. The good would not be so great a good if it were not to grow in this way through overcoming evil. Love would not be so intense if it did not have to become great enough to overcome even the ugliness in the faces of evil people. This is already being prepared for, and the pupils of this stream are being taught to recognize the necessary part evil has to play in the plan of Creation. It is there so that the great good may one day come about.

Those whose souls are being prepared by such teachings so that they will in future be able to accomplish this great educative task, are the pupils of the spiritual stream called the Manichaean school. Manichaean teaching is generally misunderstood. Anything you read or hear about it is empty talk. You may read, for instance, that the Manichees believed that the two principles of good and evil have been operating from the very beginning of the world. This is not their teaching. By 'Manichaeism' should be understood, rather, the teaching I have now described to you, its development in the future, and the pupils being prepared and guided in such a way that they can accomplish such a task in future incarnations. *Manes* is that exalted individuality repeatedly incarnated on the earth who is the guiding spirit of those whose task it is to transform evil. When we speak of the great leaders of humanity[5] we must also think of this individuality who has set himself this task. Though in present times this Manes-principle has had to fade very much into the background because of lack of understanding for the spirit, it is a wonderful and lofty principle which will win more and more pupils the more we develop an understanding for the life of spirit.

Thus you see how present-day humanity will pass over through the War of All against All into the new epoch in just the same way as the Atlantean root-race survived into our own epoch and founded our culture. After this great war, humanity will develop in seven consecutive stages. We have already seen how what is said about the opening of the seven seals in the Apocalypse of John gives us an indication of the character of the seven consecutive cultures that will follow the great war.[6] When these cultures, which in our time can only be perceived by initiates viewing the astral world and its symbolism, have run their course, a new period will begin for our earth evolution, in which new forms will once more make their appearance. And this new period, following the one just described, is symbolized in the Apocalypse of John by the sounding of the seven trumpets. Just as the epoch after the great War of All against All is characterized by the seven symbolic seals, because the seer can only perceive it from the astral perspective, so the sounding of the seven trumpets[7] characterizes the following stage of culture, because human beings can only perceive it from the perspective of the actual world of spirit, where the music of the spheres resounds. In the astral world we perceive the world in images and symbols, in devachan we perceive it in the inspirations of the music of the spheres; and this devachan is as it were the summit of what will be revealed following the great War of All against All.

If we represent this schematically, we have our seven ages of culture in the space between *a* and *b*: 1 is the ancient Indian culture, 2 the ancient Persian, 3 the Assyrian-Babylonian-Chaldean-Egyptian-Jewish, then the Graeco-Latin as fourth and our own as the fifth stage of the post-Atlantean epoch.

I II III IV V VI VII

1 2 3 4 5 6 7

a b

Figure IV would be the Atlantean epoch: *a* would be the great Flood which ends it and *b* the great War of All against All. Then follows an epoch of seven stages (VI) which is represented by the seven seals, and after this another (VII) also containing seven stages, represented by the seven trumpets. And then we reach the boundary of our physical earth evolution.

Now the Atlantean civilization (IV) which preceded our own (V) was in turn preceded by others, our own being the fifth stage of earth evolution. But we can hardly call the first a stage of civilization—everything was still delicately etheric and spiritual, so that if it had continued to develop along those lines it would never have become visible at all to sense organs such as ours. In the first stage of evolution, the sun had still not separated itself from the earth. Conditions were altogether different—we would not recognize them as similar in any way to the things of earth as we know them. Then followed a period in which the sun separated from the earth; then one in which the moon departed from it—the third stage, which we call the ancient Lemurian. At this point the human being in his very first primeval forms appeared on the earth—such grotesque forms, as I have told you, that it would shock you to have them described.[8] After the Lemurian followed the Atlantean, then finally our own.

So you see that we have on our earth seven evolutionary epochs, seven stages of evolution. The first two were absolutely unlike our epoch, the third partly ran its course in a region lying between the present Africa, Asia and Australia, in ancient Lemuria. In the very last Lemurian race there was again a small group of human beings who were most advanced. These were able to survive and migrate, and from them developed the seven Atlantean races. The fifth of the Atlantean stages gave rise to our own cultures, of which the sixth will form the basis for a future civilization after the great War of All against All. And the very last of these cultures will give rise to the one represented by the seven trumpets.

And after that? Our earth will then have reached the goal of its physical evolution. All the objects and beings upon it will then have been transformed; and to a far greater extent even than in the sixth epoch, when, as we said, people will show their good or evil qualities clearly in their faces, the human form and the form of all other beings in the seventh epoch will be a direct expression of good and of evil. All matter will bear the stamp of the spirit, nothing will be concealed in any way. Even people belonging to the sixth epoch will be unable to hide anything from those who know how to look. An evil person will express his evil, a good person will express the good within him. But in the seventh epoch it will not even be possible to use language to hide what dwells within the soul. Thought will no longer remain dumb so that it can be concealed, for what the soul thinks will reveal itself in outer resonance and echo. The condition that only the initiate knows today, in which thought resounds in devachan, will be the normal condition. But this devachan will have descended into the physical world, just as the astral world will descend into the physical world in the sixth epoch. The sixth epoch can now already be found in the astral world and the seventh in the heavenly world. The sixth epoch is the descended astral world—that is to say the reflections, the expressions, the revelations of it. The seventh epoch will be the descended heavenly world, the manifestation of it. And then the earth will have reached the goal of its physical evolution.

The earth together with all its beings will then change into an astral heavenly body. Physical substance as such will disappear. The part which has been able to spiritualize itself by that point will pass over into the spirit, into astral substance. Imagine all the beings of the earth who up to that time will have been able to express what is good, noble, intellectual and beautiful in their external, material form, who will bear an impression of Christ Jesus in their countenances, who in their words will give expression to Christ Jesus, whose thoughts will sound forth and be manifest—all these will have the power to dissolve what they have within them as physical matter, in the same way that warm water dissolves salt. Everything physical will pass over into an astral heavenly globe. But those elements which have not progressed so far as to be a material and corporeal manifestation of what is noble, beautiful, intellectual and good, will not have the power to dissolve matter; for them matter will remain—they will retain material form and become hardened in matter. At this point in the earth's evolution will occur an ascent into worlds of spirit of forms which will live in the astral and which will expel from themselves another material sphere, one containing beings unfit for the ascent because they are unable to dissolve what is of material nature.

In this way our earth will advance towards its future, its substance growing ever finer and more subtle. The soul will gradually refine this matter from within, until it develops the power to dissolve it. Then will come the time when the insoluble element will be ejected as a separate cosmic globe. In the course of seven ages what has hardened itself in matter will be driven out, and the power which causes this will be an opposite force to that which will have sublimated the good forces, driven them to ascend.

And what will lead to the dissolution of matter? The power of love gained through the Christ-principle. Beings become capable of dissolving matter through taking love into their souls. The more the soul is warmed by love the more powerfully will it be able to work upon matter, spiritualizing, astralizing the whole earth and transforming it into an astral globe. But just as love dissolves matter, like warm water dissolving salt, so will the opposite of love bear down, again through seven stages, upon everything which has not developed the capacity to fulfil the earth's mission.

The opposite of divine love is called divine wrath—that is the technical expression for it. In the same way that humanity was imbued with love during the course of the fourth cultural epoch, a love that will become ever warmer through the last stages of our time, the sixth and seventh, so the opposite principle which hardens matter around itself is also growing. Its effect—the expulsion of matter—is indicated in the Apocalypse of John by the outpouring of the seven vials of divine wrath.[9] Just imagine this, quite pictorially: the substance of the earth will become ever finer, the substance of the human being also will become more and more spiritual, and within the refined parts only the the coarsest elements will still be visible, like sloughed snake-skins or the shells of snails.

These harder parts will become more and more attached to the self-refining substance. Viewing the last epoch, that of the sounding trumpets, with spiritual vision, you would see that people consist of delicate spiritualized bodies; and that those who have hardened and compacted the material principle within themselves have preserved within themselves the most substantial constituents of matter; and that this will fall as husks to compose the material globe which will remain after the epoch represented by the sounding of the trumpets.

This is prophetically described in the Apocalypse of John, and it is important to develop a feeling in our souls for this knowledge of what is coming, so that it may fire our will. What will we have made of ourselves by the time the sixth and seventh epochs are over? What will we have made of our body? The human body today, as we can observe, is not yet the expression and manifestation of what the soul experiences within, but it will more and more become so. The outer human form will become an expression of the good to the extent that we receive the highest, most exalted teaching there is on this earth—the message of Jesus Christ. The highest teaching that can be given us is that of Jesus Christ. We must take it up into ourselves, must make it our own, and not only with our powers of understanding. We must take it into our inmost being, just as we take nourishment into the physical body. As humanity develops through this cultural epoch it will take up this joyful message more and more inwardly, and will have to regard its receptivity to this teaching of love as the ultimate aim of the mission of the earth. The power of love in its widest scope is contained in the Gospels, in the 'book', and the seer cannot do otherwise than say: In spirit I see a future time when what is in the Gospels will no longer be externalized in a book, but will have been ingested by the human being, will have become internalized.[10]

Our earthly evolution depends upon two things. This earth was preceded by what we call the cosmos of wisdom, which in turn was preceded by what we call the cosmos of strength or power—such a concept does not, it is true, have much resonance, but we must use it because that is how it is known. Wisdom and strength have been received as a heritage from previous stages of evolution, from the ancient Moon and Sun stages. This, we can see, comes to expression within our own earth evolution in the fact that we name its first half after Mars, the representative of the sun-forces. All that we need to be aware of at this point is that Mars is what implanted iron into earthly evolution. Mars is for us the bringer of strength. The second half of earth evolution, in contrast, stands under the sway of Mercury, representative of ancient Moon evolution which incorporated wisdom into the earth, the legacy of this Moon stage. Earth evolution therefore consists of two parts, Mars and Mercury, which have mediated the legacy of two mighty forces: the inheritance from the cosmos of strength is expressed in Mars, the inheritance from the cosmos of wisdom is expressed in Mercury. The mission of the earth itself is to add love to these. Love is to be made gloriously manifest through earth evolution. This is the very profound thought expressed by the writer of the Apocalypse, and one linked to the whole of the rest of earthly evolution. (See the fourth occult seal picture.)

Return with me once more to the most ancient period of Atlantean times, to the time we described by saying that the air was still saturated with water. The human being was still a water-creature. Not until the middle of the Atlantean epoch did he progress far enough to leave the water and tread solid ground. Up to the middle of earthly evolution we must regard water as the medium of evolution, thereafter the solid earth came into its own. It is only half the truth if we speak of Atlantis as consisting of dry land—it was not so much covered by ocean as by an in-between element, rather like air saturated with water. This water-air was the element in which human beings lived. Only later did they develop the capacity to live in pure air and stand on *terra firma*. That was comparatively speaking not so long ago, and if we survey the whole evolution of the earth we can say, symbolically, that there are two principles and forces at work: water, up until the midpoint of evolution on the one hand, and earth on the other. Up to the middle of the fourth epoch the Mars forces hold sway, the water-forces so to speak; and thereafter the Mercury forces are dominant, when the solid earth suports human life. This fits perfectly with the idea that we are supported in our entire earthly mission by two pillars, which you saw symbolically represented in the congress hall in Munich.[11] These represent two parts of the earth's mission, the two legacies the human being has received from earlier stages. And above them is symbolically represented what is to be attained through the earth itself: love, revealing itself in glory, supported by the two legacies from the past.

The writer of the Apocalypse really describes exactly what can be perceived by one who ascends into spiritual realms. And so when we observe what lies beyond the end of earth evolution when earthly substance dissolves into spirit, we find it symbolically portrayed in the fourth occult seal. We see the two forces which the earth has received as legacy from the cosmos of wisdom and the cosmos of strength, and we see all that appears as the fulfilment of the earth's mission, as the force of love which the human being develops. The whole image appears to us as the symbolic personification and embodiment of the human being of the future, supported by these two forces, permeated by the power of love. The message of love, the book before him, is a book which not only influences him from without but which he has to ingest. Here we behold the mighty picture which now appears: 'And I saw another mighty angel'—that is, a being who appears as such because he has already reached a stage higher than that of present humanity—'descend from the spiritual spheres'—this is how it is perceived by the seer—'clothed with a cloud, and his countenance was as it were the sun and his feet as pillars of fire'—these pillars are the two forces of which we have spoken, which the earth received as a legacy—'And he had in his hand a little book open; and his right foot was set upon the sea and his left upon the earth... And I said unto him, Give me the little book. And he said unto me, Take it and eat it up; and it shall make thy belly bitter, but in thy mouth it shall be sweet as honey. And I took the little book from the hand of the angel and ate it up; and it was in my mouth sweet as honey.'

Here we have an accurate description of the feeling which arises in the seer when he directs his gaze to the point when the earth passes from a physical, material condition into the astrally spiritual, when the earth mission is attained. And when the seer perceives this he learns what is really connected with this message of love, whose impulse entered in the fourth cultural epoch: he learns in his present life, as the writer of the Apocalypse learned, what bliss is, and what bliss lies in store for humanity. But he learns of it in his present physical condition; for a being desiring to live together with human beings would have to incarnate physically. And in many respects it is just because the present human body offers the spirit the possibility of ascending to great heights that it also gives the possibility of suffering. So while the soul of the seer, of the one who perceives the Apocalypse, is able to ascend into spiritual regions to receive the Gospel of love, and in spirit is able to feel the bliss sweet as honey, yet his present-day body compels him to recognize that his spiritual ascent also produces in this body the antithesis of that bliss. He expresses this by saying that although the little book is at first as sweet as honey, it gives him severe pains in the belly once he has swallowed it. But that is only a small reflection of the 'crucifixion in the body'. The higher the spirit rises, the harder it is for it to dwell in the body, and the symbolic expression for such pain is this 'crucifixion in the body'.

This is, then, a brief sketch of what will happen in the course of our earthly evolution, what lies before us as we evolve. We have described this up to the point at which the human being is transformed into an astral being, when the best parts of the earth cease to be physical and pass over into a spiritual condition, when only one isolated part will be separated off and fall away into the abyss through the power of divine wrath. And we shall see that even then the last stage has not yet been reached, that salvation would still be possible for this cast-off portion of earth-evolution, although what takes shape in the abyss is pictured in the most frightful symbols: the seven-headed and ten-horned beast, and the two-horned beast.[12]

Notes

GA = German edition of collected works of Rudolf Steiner. English editions are available through Rudolf Steiner Press, UK, and Anthroposophic Press, USA.

Editor's Introduction

1. Haag, H.: *Abschied vom Teufel. Vom christlichen Umgang mit dem Bösen*, Zurich, 1990.
2. Schroeder, H.-W.: *Der Mensch und das Böse. Ursprung, Wesen und Sinn der Wiedersachermächte*, Stuttgart, 1984.
3. Developing a moral impulse (moral intuition) out of the actual and immediate situation, without relying on a previously formed categorical imperative, is also the central theme of Rudolf Steiner's fundamental work, *The Philosophy of Spiritual Activity* (Rudolf Steiner Press, 1992, translated and revised by Rita Stebbing).
4. Such an inner Manichaeism, though not called such, can be seen as a deep stratum in the psychotherapeutic approach of Jung (Jung, C.G.: *Bewusstes und Unbewusstes*, Frankfurt am Main, 1978; Beck, I.: *Das Problem des Bösen und seine Bewältigung*, Munich, 1976).
5. Häring, H.: *Das Problem des Bösen in der Theologie*, Darmstadt, 1985.

Part I Chapter 1

1. Cf., *Wahrspruchworte*, GA 40, page 93.
2. *Geisteswissenschaft als Lebensgut*, GA 63.
3. To the Greek school of the *Stoics* (4th–3rd century BC), belonged such philosophers as Zenon of Kition, Kleanthes and Chrysippus. They derived their name from the hall of columns in Athens, the Stoa.

4. *The Riddles of Philosophy*, Anthroposophic Press, New York, 1973. GA 18, 1914.
5. Cf. *Confessions*, book 7, chapters 12–16.
6. R.J. Campbell: *The New Theology*, 1910.
7. Plotinus, AD205–270, the most important neo-Platonist. He was born in Egypt and later lived in Rome.
8. Nakae Toju, *The wise man of Omi*, 1605–78. He adapted the teachings of the Chinese sage Wang Yang-Ming to make them suited to the cultural life of Japan.
9. Hermann Lotze, Professor of philosophy from 1844. *Mikrokosmos, Ideen zur Naturgeschichte und Geschichte der Menschheit*, 1856–64, vol. 3, book 9, chapter 5, pages 609–11. There is more about Lotze in Rudolf Steiner's *The Riddles of Philosophy*, GA 18, in the chapter 'Modern Idealistic World-views'.
10. Jacob Boehme, 1575–1624.
11. 'Die Sittliche Grundlage des Menschen', 12 December 1914, Berlin (in GA 63). This lecture deals with the spiritual origin of conscience.
12. Cf., for example, the lecture of 30 October 1913: 'Die geistige Welt und die Geisteswissenschaft. Ausblicke und Ziele der Gegenwart' in GA 63 (*The Dramatic Art of the Goetheanum*, Rudolf Steiner Publishing Co.).
13. Angelus Silesius. The extract quoted here by Rudolf Steiner actually comes from a poem by Friedrich Rückert, 'World and I', and is a free rendering of the following epigram by Silesius:

    No why or wherefore has the rose, it blooms because it blossoms,
    It dwells not on itself, oblivious to whether anyone sees it.
    Cherubinischer Wandersmann, Book 1, aphorism 289
14. 'Zwischen Tod und Wiedergeburt des Menschen', Berlin, 19 March 1914, in GA 63 (*Life Beyond Death*, Rudolf Steiner Press, 1995).
15. Arthur Schopenhauer, 1788–1860.
16. Eduard v. Hartmann, 1842–1906.
17. Philipp Mainländer: *Philosophy of Redemption*, 1876.
18. Max Seiling, *Ein neuer Messias*, 1888.
19. J.F.A. Bahnsen, 1830–81, who lived in Lauenburg/Holstein.
20. Mephistopheles in *Faust* 1, verse 1936–39. Translation M. Barton.

Part I Chapter 2

1. Immanuel Kant, *The Critique of Pure Reason*, 1781, 2nd book. This was the chief work of transcendental Dialectics.
2. *The World as Will and Idea*, book 3, section 52.
3. Goethe: *The Metamorphosis of Plants*. Vol. 1 of *Goethe's Scientific Writings* (1883–97), GA 1a.
4. Cf. the further indications about this in lecture 6, GA 134, as well as lecture 13, 'Theosophy and Rosicrucianism', in *Menschheitsentwicklung and Christus-Erkenntnis* ('Human Evolution and Knowledge of Christ') (22 lectures, Kassel and Basel, 1907), GA 100.

Part II Chapter 1

1. Between August 1922 and September 1924, Steiner gave roughly 110 lectures, covering all sorts of different subjects, for the workers at the Goetheanum. He often responded directly and spontaneously to questions which his audience asked. In the months preceding this particular lecture he had discussed and given practical, detailed examples of such themes as the nature and 'bodies' of the human being, waking, dreaming and sleeping, life and death, reincarnation and questions of Christology (GA 349) and health and illness (GA 348). It is noticeable that in these lectures he employed a rather different mode of expression to that used in other lectures: richer in imagery and colloquialism. Any separate statement must, even more than elsewhere in his work, be seen in these lectures in its context within the whole inner structure of his train of thought, and in relation to the particular nature of his audience. Extracting isolated quotes or passages from this context might well lead to misinterpretation or misunderstanding.
2. Lecture of 21 April 1923 (about, among other things, the two Jesus children) in GA 9.
3. A great wooden sculpture of the 'Representative of Humanity' between Lucifer and Ahriman was planned to be installed in the first Goetheanum, which was built entirely of wood. At the time the building burnt down, on New Year's Eve 1922, the sculp-

ture had not yet been completed or installed, and so escaped destruction. It can still be seen today in the second Goetheanum.

4. Last lecture in GA 349, on 9 May 1923.

Part II Chapter 2

1. Cf. lectures 1–9 in: *Die Polarität von Dauer und Entwicklung im Menschenleben* (The Polarity Between Duration and Evolution in Human Life), GA 184, given between 6 and 22 September 1918 in Dornach.
2. Cf. lecture 3 in the same cycle, GA 184.
3. Cf. the lectures of 27–29 September 1918 in vol. 2 of *Geisteswissenschaftliche Erläuterungen zu Goethes 'Faust'. Das Faust-Problem. Die romantische und die klassische Walpurgisnacht* (Spiritual-scientific explanations of Goethe's *Faust*. The Faust-problem. The Romantic and Classical Walpurgis Night), GA 273.
4. Cf. in this connection the essay 'The Relationship of the Luciferic and the Ahrimanic to the Human Being' in *Philosophy and Anthroposophy*, Mercury Press, 1988, GA 35 (1918).
5. Gottfried Wilhelm Leibniz (1646–1716). The editor was unable to trace the source of this anecdote.
6. Cf. lectures 5 and 8 in the same cycle, GA 184.

Part III Chapter 1

1. In the previous lecture, Steiner spoke about the different stages of consciousness which came to expression in the ancient Indian, Chaldean, Greek and Germanic cultures. He shed light on the actual spiritual realities underlying the figures of the Germanic gods. In 'Brahma', the ancient Indian worshipped the founding primal being of all existence, whose chief characteristic is 'creative knowledge' (cf. also 'Germanic and Indian Occult Teachings', 8 March 1906, in *Die Weltratsel und die Anthroposophie* (The Riddles of the World and Anthroposophy), GA 54. 'Atma(n)' is the highest capacity that the

human being can develop, standing even higher than 'budhi' (transformed etheric body) and 'manas' (transformed astral body), and corresponding to the transformation of the physical body; at the same time it represents a person's inmost, immortal essence. Rudolf Steiner's terms for these three stages were spirit-man, life-spirit and spirit-self.

2. For more information on the concepts of Lemurian, Atlantean etc. epochs, see *Occult Science—An Outline*, Rudolf Steiner Press, 1969, GA 13.
3. E.g., Matthew 4, 10 and Luke 22, 3.
4. For more about the devas, see the lecture given in Berlin on 8 October 1905, in *Grundelement der Esoterik* (Basic Elements of Esotericism), GA 93a. The devas are 'descendants' of the angelic hierarchies, whose task is to be 'planetary spirits', 'angels of the earth's orbit', group souls and folk spirits.
5. Cf. the lecture of 8 August 1908 in *Universe, Earth and Man*, Rudolf Steiner Press, 1987, GA 105.
6. *The Manifestations of Karma*. Eleven lectures given in Hamburg, May 1910 (Rudolf Steiner Press, 1995), GA 120.
7. Lecture of 29 February 1912, 'Der Tod bei Mensch, Tier und Pflanze' (Death in the Human, Animal and Plant), in *Menschengeschichte im Lichte der Geistesforschung* (Human History in the Light of Spiritual Research), GA 61.
8. Cf. the lecture of 25 June 1922 in *Human Questions and Cosmic Answers*, Rudolf Steiner Press, 1960, GA 213.
9. Cf. also the lecture of 2 April 1915 in *Wege der geistigen Erkenntnis und der Erneuerung künstlerischer Weltanschauung* (Paths of Spiritual Knowledge and of Renewal of an Artistic World-view), GA 161.
10. Lecture of 11 August 1908 in *Universe, Earth and Man*, GA 105; lecture of 22 August 1911 in *Wonders of the World*, Rudolf Steiner Press, 1983, GA 129.
11. See lecture of 1 May 1909: 'Alteuropäisches Hellsehen' (Ancient European Clairvoyance) in *Wo und wie findet man den Geist?* (Where and How do we Find the Spirit?), GA 57.
12. See Matthew 3, 2 and Mark 1, 15.
13. For more on Odin, Thor and other gods of Germanic mythology, see lecture 8 in the same cycle, GA 121.

Part III Chapter 2

1. The previous lecture in this cycle dealt with the contrast between the old traditions of oriental wisdom, which faded into a withered form in Roman times, and whose echoes reverberated on into the philosophy and theology of medieval times, and the youthful, vigorous soul-life that was still untutored and unknowing, but from which unfolded our ego-evolution. In the folk-migration period, these two elements encountered and penetrated one another in Italy, Spain, France and England. This contrast between dying knowledge and unknowing life is the starting point of the lecture.
2. E.g., August 1910 in *Genesis*, GA 122; 29 May 1908 in *The Gospel of St John*, GA 103; and 7 May 1912 in *Erfahrungen des Übersinnlichen* (Experiencing Supersensible Realms), GA 143.
3. Yahveh (Jehovah) is the guiding being of the exusiai, mentioned in the last lecture of Part II of this book.
4. In the sixth lecture of the cycle *Secrets of the Threshold*, Anthroposophic Press, New York, 1987, GA 147.
5. Particularly in the second lecture of the cycle referred to in the previous note.
6. For example, in the second lecture of the cycle *Kunst- und Lebensfragen im Lichte der Geisteswissenschaft* (Art and Life Questions in the Light of the Science of the Spirit), GA 162, from which this lecture is taken.
7. In a different shorthand transcript of this lecture, instead of the word 'general' (im Allgemeinen), the word 'etheric body' (Im Ätherleibe) is given. The first version was chosen, as it seemed to make sense of the following sentences; however the second would also make sense within the overall context.
8. The 'Representative of Man', which was not completed at the time of the fire that destroyed the First Goetheanum, and therefore survived.

Part IV Chapter 1

1. Cf. the lectures of 15 and 30 October 1916, in *Goethe und die Krisis des neunzehnten Jahrhunderts* (Goethe and the Crisis of the

Nineteenth Century), GA 171; and the lectures of 18, 19 and 26 November 1916 in *The Karma of Vocation*, Anthroposophic Press, New York, 1984, GA 172.

2. The lecture of the previous day dealt, among other things, with the role of the bourgeoisie in the nineteenth century, and the development of liberal ideas—which in fact missed the opportunity for developing an approach and understanding prepared to penetrate reality by remaining abstract.
3. *Occult Science—An Outline*, Rudolf Steiner Press, 1969.
4. See note 1, chapter 5.
5. This lecture was given during the First World War. The Austro-Hungarian Empire had recently collapsed. At the beginning of October, the German government had offered a cease-fire to the American president Woodrow Wilson (1856–1924) on the basis of his 'Fourteen Points', which he announced on 8 January 1918. Included in these was a sentence about the 'self-determination of nations'.
6. Cf. the lectures from 31 August to 2 September 1918 [in English typescript No. Z271 in the library at Rudolf Steiner House] in *Die Wissenschaft vom Werden des Menschen. Das Walten der kosmischen Vernunft im Sprachenstehen*, GA 183.
7. E.g., in the public lectures of 14 March 1918 in Berlin, 'Das geschichtliche Leben der Menschheit und seine Rätsel' (The History of Humanity and its Riddles), in *Das Ewige in der Menschenseele. Unsterblichkeit und Freiheit* (The Eternal in the Human Soul. Immortality and Freedom), GA 67; and in the lecture of 30 March 1918 in *Erdensterben und Weltenleben. Anthroposophische Lebensgaben. Bewusstseinsnotwendigkeiten für Gegenwart und Zukunft* (Earth-death and Cosmic Life. Anthroposophical Gifts to Life. Consciousness necessary for the Present and Future), GA 181.
8. Woodrow Wilson, 1856–1924, president of the USA from 1912–20.
9. 17 October 1918: 'Die Geschichte der Neuzeit im Lichte der geisteswissenschaftlichen Forschung' (Modern History in the light of Spiritual-scientific Research), in *Die Ergänzung heutiger Wissenschaft durch Anthpoposophie* (Extending Modern Science through Anthroposophy), GA 73.
10. See note 1.

11. Ernst Horneffer, born 1871, succeeded Dr Fritz Kögel as editor in the Nietzsche archives.

Part IV Chapter 2

1. See particularly *Kosmische und menschliche Geschichte* (Cosmic and Human History), 6 volumes, Dornach, various dates (GA 170–174b), parts of which are available in English in *The Riddle of Humanity: the Spiritual Background of Human History*, Rudolf Steiner Press, London, 1990; *Inner Impulses of Human Evolution. The Mexican Mysteries and the Knights Templar*, Anthroposophic Press, New York, 1984; *The Karma of Vocation*, Anthroposophic Press, New York, 1984; *The Karma of Untruthfulness*, Rudolf Steiner Press, London, vol. 1, 1988, vol. 2, 1992; *The Mission of the Archangel Michael*, Anthroposophic Press, New York, 1961, as well as other lectures from 1917 to 1919.
2. See *Towards Social Renewal*, Rudolf Steiner Press, London, 1977.
3. Cf. Rudolf Steiner's descriptions of various initiation centres (oracles) in Atlantis, particularly the Vulcan, Mercury and Venus oracles; in: *Occult Science—An Outline*, Rudolf Steiner Press, 1969.
4. The expression 'Aryan' may cause offence. But it is important to bear in mind exactly what Rudolf Steiner, following theosophical terminology, meant by the concept of 'race'. He saw it in terms of stages of evolution which all humanity passes through. In this way the whole post-Atlantean epoch corresponds to the 'fifth root-race', the 'Aryan' (*Cosmic Memory*, chapters 2 and 3, GA 11). The root-races are in turn subdivided into sub-races or evolutionary epochs. Absolutely no qualitative judgements about individuals are intended by these terms, for concepts of race and soul-evolution are quite separate and distinct.
5. Plato, *Phaedrus* (242).
6. The Theosophical Society, founded in 1875 in New York, moved its headquarters a few years later to Adyar, near Madras, in India. In her first work, *Isis Unveiled*, its founder H.P. Blavatsky still adhered to western occultism, but as time went

on she increasingly turned to Indian wisdom. See Rudolf Steiner, *The Occult Movement in the Nineteenth Century*, Rudolf Steiner Press, London, 1973.

7. John Locke (1632–1704), English philosopher. David Hume (1711–76), Scottish philosopher, historian, economist and essayist. John Stuart Mill (1806–73), English philosopher and economist. Herbert Spencer (1820–1903), English philosopher. Charles Robert Darwin (1802–82), English naturalist, first soundly established the theory of organic evolution in his monumental work *The Origin of Species*.
8. Georg Hegel (1770–1831), Johann Gottlieb Fichte (1762–1814), Wilhelm von Schelling (1775–1854) were some of the great German philosophers of the eighteenth–nineteenth centuries. Cf. Rudolf Steiner, *The Riddles of Philosophy*, Anthroposophic Press, New York, 1973.
9. Wilhelm von Humboldt (1767–1835), German philologist, diplomat and man of letters. His work, cited here, was completed in 1851. A literal translation of its title would be 'Ideas for an attempt to determine the limits of the sphere of influence of the state'.
10. *Friedrich Nietzsche. Fighter for Freedom*, Rudolf Steiner Publishers, New Jersey, 1960.
11. Hermann Grimm (1828–1901). The quotation comes from his essay 'Heinrich von Treitschkes Deutsche Geschichte' in *Beiträge zur deutschen Kulturgeschichte*, Berlin, 1897.
12. See *The Complete Works of Friedrich Nietzsche*, vol. 1, 'The Birth of Tragedy, or Hellenism and Pessimism'.
13. *Asuras*: see Rudolf Steiner, *Geisteswissenschaftliche Menschenkunde*, Dornach, 1979, GA 107, lecture of 22 March 1909 in Berlin. This lecture is in English translation in *The Deed of Christ and the Opposing Spiritual Powers*, Steiner Book Centre, Vancouver, 1976.

Part V Chapter 1

1. 'The Work of the Angels in Man's Astral Body', Zurich, 9 October 1918 in the same cycle, *Der Tod als Lebenswandlung* (Death as Transformation of Life), GA 182.

2. GA 8.
3. Adolf Harnack, 1851–1930.
4. E.g., 'Drei Wege der Seele zu Christus' (Three-Soul-paths to Christ), 16–17 April 1912, in *Erfahrungen des Übersinnlichen* (Experiencing Supersensible Realms), GA 143.
5. Tertullian, theological writer from AD160 to 220. His work in defence of the Christians is entitled 'Apologeticum'.
6. Tertullian in *De Carne Christi* (according to Willmann, *Geschichte des Idealismus*).
7. Cf. chapter 13, verse 18 of Revelations.
8. Justinian, 527–565, Emperor over the East Roman regions.
9. Zeno Isauricus, Caesar from 474 to 491. Closed down the school at Odessa in 489.
10. Mohammed, 570–632.
11. It is not quite clear what this means. The German text speaks of a 'Zarathustra-Impuls zur Unzeit', to which the German editor has appended a footnote as follows:
    'This might either be the renewal of ancient Persian fire-cults at this time, or could also be connected with impulses originating with the Zarathustra individuality, which perhaps reappeared in a distorted form.'
12. Paul, in II Corinthians 12, 7 says: 'And lest I should be exalted above measure through the abundance of the revelations, there was given to me a thorn in the flesh, the messenger of Satan to buffet me, lest I should be exalted above measure.' This 'thorn' of God-denial, of which Steiner speaks, therefore also has a positive aspect.
13. In the *Canones contra Photium* of this Council held to oppose the patriarch Photius, Canon 11 ordains that the human being does not have 'two souls', but 'unam animam rationabilem et intellectualem'—one rational and intellectual soul. Cf. also Steiner's references to the Council of Constantinople, GA nos. 174a, 174b, 191, 194, 203.
14. Angelus Silesius (Johann Scheffler), 1644–77. From the *Cherubinischer Wandersmann* (The Cherubic Wanderer).
15. See note 3.
16. Johannes Müller, 1864–1949, a 'philosopher of life' who directed a 'Free Institute of Personal Life for Seekers of all Persuasion and Background' at Schloss Elmau in Upper

Bavaria. He was the author of numerous writings on social and religious problems.

17. Friedrich Schiller in *Tabulae Votivae.*
18. See Rudolf Steiner, *Eurythmie. Die Offenbarung der sprechenden Seele* (Eurythmy, Revealing the Speaking Soul), GA 277.
19. In the lecture of 17 October 1918, 'Die Geschichte der Neuzeit im Lichte geisteswissenschaftlicher Forschung' (The History of Recent Times in the light of Spiritual-scientific Research) in *Die Ergänzung heutiger Wissenschaften durch Anthroposophie* (Anthroposophy's Contribution to the Modern Sciences), public lectures held in Zurich between 1917 and 1918, GA 73. The present theme was taken up again in the 'questions-and-answers' of this lecture.
20. *Mere Literature and other Essays*, 1896.
21. Herman Grimm, 1838–1901, art historian. For other comparisons Steiner made between Grimm and Wilson, see also the seventh lecture of this volume and the lecture of 30 March 1918, Berlin, in *Erdensterben und Weltenleben. Anthroposophische Lebensgaben. Bewusstseins-Notwendigkeiten für Gegenwart und Zukunft* (Earth-death and Cosmic Life. Anthroposophical Gifts for Life. Demands of Consciousness for Present and Future Times), GA 181.
22. II Corinthians, chapters 3, 6.

Part V Chapter 2

1. See also lectures 4 and 7 of the same cycle (*The Apocalypse of St John*), GA 104. The War of All against All will not take place until after the end of the seventh cultural epoch—in approx. 5,900 years.
2. These are illustrated in *The Apocalypse of St John*, Rudolf Steiner Press, 1977.
3. The 'Slavic' and the 'American' cultural epochs.
4. For more about the seven 'races' of Atlantis, see *Cosmic Memory*, GA 11, chapter 2. The fifth Atlantean race was that of the 'ancient Semites'—one can, in this context, think of Noah's three sons, *Sem*, *Ham* and *Japhet*.
5. For more about Manichaeism, see also the ninth lecture in *The*

East in the Light of the West, GA 113, Rudolf Steiner Publishing Co., London, and Anthroposophic Press, New York, 1940; and the ninth lecture in *Occult Reading and Occult Hearing*, GA 156; also H. Reimann, *Manichäismus—das Christentum der Freiheit* (Manichaeism—the Christianity of Freedom), Dornach, 1980, in which is shown the inner connection of ancient Christian streams, including Manichaeism, with later 'heretic movements' such as the Cathars, the Masons of the late Middle Ages and the Rosicrucians. All these movements were suppressed and sidelined by the Church. But the three ideals of the French Revolution can be traced back to this 'Christianity of Freedom' of the early Christian centuries.

6. Cf. the fourth lecture of the same cycle, GA 104.
7. Revelations, 8, 6–11, 19.
8. Cf. the sixth lecture of the same cycle, GA 104.
9. Revelations, 16.
10. See Revelations, 10, 8–11.
11. See Rudolf Steiner, *Bilder okkulter Siegel und Säulen. Der Münchner Kongress Pfingsten 1907 und seine Auswirkungen* (Pictures of Occult Seals and Pillars. The Munich Congress of Whitsun 1907 and its Effects), GA 284/85, 1977.
12. About the seven-headed and ten-horned beast, see the ninth lecture of the same cycle; and about the two-horned beast see lectures 11–12, GA 104.

Sources of the Lectures by Rudolf Steiner

'Evil Illumined through the Science of the Spirit'. Not previously translated. German = GA 63.

'Good and Evil: Creation and Death'. In: *The World of the Senses and the World of the Spirit*, Steiner Book Centre, North Vancouver, 1979. German = GA 134.

'Christ, Ahriman and Lucifer in Relationship to the Human Being'. Not previously translated. German = GA 349.

'The Relation of Ahrimanic and Luciferic Beings to the Normally Evolved Hierarchies'. In: *The Three Streams of Human Evolution*, Rudolf Steiner Press, London, 1965. German = GA 184.

'The Migard Snake, the Fenris Wolf and Hel'. In: *The Mission of the Individual Folk Souls*, Rudolf Steiner Press, London, 1970. German = GA 121.

'The Tree of Life, and the Tree of Knowledge of Good and Evil'. Not previously translated. German = GA 162.

'Supersensible Aspects of Historical Research'. In: *From Symptom to Reality in Modern History*, Rudolf Steiner Press, London, 1976. German = GA 185.

'The Three Streams of Materialistic Civilization'. In: *Ideas for a New Europe*, Rudolf Steiner Press, London 1992. German = GA 194.

'How Do I Find the Christ?'. In: *How Do I Find the Christ?*, Anthroposophic Press/Rudolf Steiner Press, New York/London 1941. German = GA 182.

'The Future of Human Evolution'. In: *The Apocalypse of St. John*, Rudolf Steiner Press, London, 1977. German = GA 104.

In the same series:

Nature Spirits
ISBN 1 855840 18 9; 208pp; £11.95

Self Transformation
ISBN 1 855840 19 7; 256pp; £12.95

Life Beyond Death
ISBN 1 855840 17 0; 256pp; £12.95

Angels
ISBN 1 855840 060 X; 192pp; £10.95